EXILE
AND RETURN

THE BIBLE
AND
ITS STORY

Planned and produced by
Jaca Book — Le Centurion
from the ideas of
Charles Ehlinger, Hervé Lauriot Prévost,
Pierre Talec, and the editorial committee
of Jaca Book

A chapter outline for this volume
is printed on the last two pages
of the volume.

EXILE
AND RETURN

THE BIBLE AND ITS STORY

Text by Enrico Galbiati, Elio Guerriero, Antonio Sicari
Translation by Kenneth D. Whitehead
Illustrations by Sandro Corsi, Sergio Molino, Franco Vignazia

 Winston Press 430 Oak Grove Minneapolis, Minnesota 55403

Published in Italy under the title
Esilia, Ritorno, Giudaismo
Copyright © 1983 Jaca Book—Le Centurion

**Licensed publisher and distributor
of the English-language edition:**
    Winston Press, Inc.
    430 Oak Grove
    Minneapolis, Minnesota 55403
    United States of America

Agents:
Canada—
LeDroit/Novalis-Select
135 Nelson Street
Ottawa, Ontario
Canada K1N 7R4

Australia, New Zealand, New Guinea, Fiji Islands—
Dove Communications, Pty. Ltd.
Suite 1 60-64 Railway Road
Blackburn, Victoria 3130
Australia

Acknowledgments:
All Scripture quotations, unless otherwise indicated,
are taken from the Revised Standard Version Common
Bible, copyright © 1973 by the Division of Christian
Education of the National Council of the Churches of
Christ in U.S.A. Used by permission.

All Scripture quotations indicated by *TEV* (Today's
English Version) are from the *Good News Bible*—Old
Testament: Copyright © American Bible Society 1976;
New Testament: Copyright © American Bible Society,
1966, 1971, 1976.

Winston Scriptural Consultant:
Catherine Litecky, CSJ
Department of Theology
College of St. Catherine
St. Paul, Minnesota

Winston Staff:
Lois Welshons, Hermann Weinlick—editorial
Reg Sandland, Kathe Wilcoxon—design

Jaca Book—Le Centurion Editorial Committee:
François Brossinger, Maretta Campi, Charles Ehlinger,
Enrico Galbiati, Elio Guerriero, Pierre Talec

Color selection: Carlo Scotti, Milan
Printing: Gorenjski tisk, Kranj, Yugoslavia

Copyright © 1984, English-language edition,
Jaca Book—Le Centurion. All rights reserved.
Printed in Yugoslavia.

Library of Congress Catalog Card Number: 83-50140
ISBN: 0-86683-195-9

Introduction
EXILE
AND RETURN

In exile in Babylon after the capture of Jerusalem and the destruction of the Temple in 587 B.C., the Jews thought their world had collapsed. Torn away from all they held dear, the exiles felt that God had abandoned them. Mournfully they sang in Babylon, "How can I sing a song of the Lord in a foreign land?" (Psalm 137)

Many years later the Jews came to realize that the Exile was a time of purification and deepening of their religion. God took them away from the externals of their religion and through the prophets guided them to a religion based on greater sincerity of heart.

Mighty Babylon in its turn experienced defeat by the Persians, whose king, Cyrus, allowed the exiled Jews to return home. Those who returned struggled to rebuild Jerusalem and the Temple. They tried to preserve Jewish identity and religion from powerful foreign influences and pressures. One of the strongest threats to Judaism came from Hellenism, a way of life based on Greek language and culture, which Alexander the Great forced on the nations he conquered.

During this period the Jews fought wars against more powerful enemies and usually lost. In spite of this, Jewish authors managed to write a variety of books included in the Bible as "wisdom" writings. Some of these books gave encouragement to those enduring persecution; others tried to answer questions such as, Why do good people suffer?

No matter how difficult things got for the Jews, they continued to trust that God was watching over them. Their hope focused on a future Messiah, an ideal king from the family of David, who would defeat Israel's enemies and establish a kingdom of justice, peace, and love.

Catherine Litecky

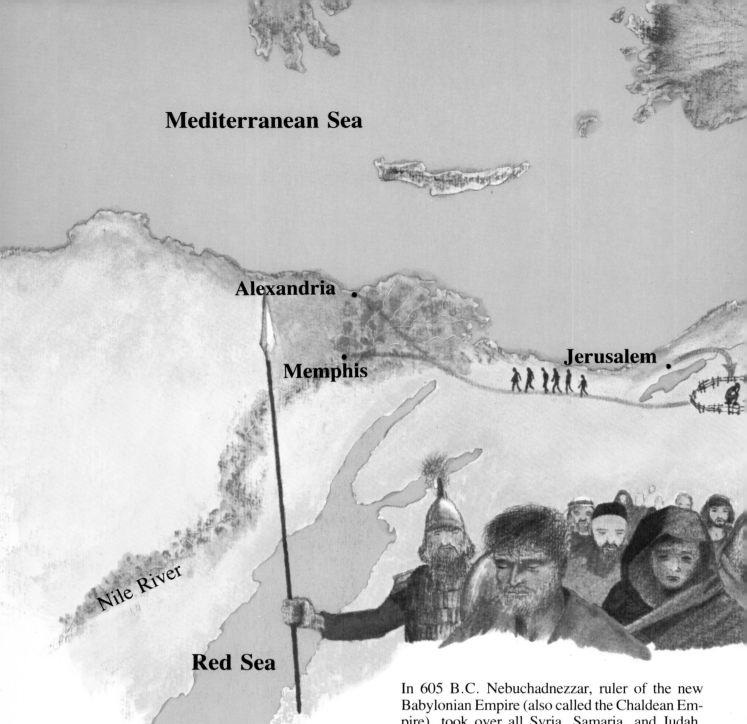

Mediterranean Sea

Alexandria •

Memphis •

Jerusalem •

Nile River

Red Sea

1 The kingdom of Judah came
to an end in 587 B.C.
The Babylonian army
captured Jerusalem
and destroyed the Temple.
Many people were sent
into exile in Babylonia.

In 605 B.C. Nebuchadnezzar, ruler of the new
Babylonian Empire (also called the Chaldean Empire), took over all Syria, Samaria, and Judah.
The king of Judah, Jehoiakim (609-598), was
subject to this Babylonian sovereign and was supposed to pay an annual tribute to him. He refused
to pay it, and as a consequence the Babylonians
sent an army against him. The Babylonian army
mounted a siege against Jerusalem in 597 B.C.
Meanwhile, Jehoiakim had died and had been
succeeded by his youngest son, Jehoiachin (598-
597). He was able to withstand the Babylonian
siege for about three months; then he finally surrendered and was carried off to Babylonia. Judah's leaders and army officers were taken to
Babylonia at this same time; in all, about seven
thousand leading citizens, along with some one
thousand skilled artisans, were deported. The most
precious of the Temple and palace furnishings were
also carried off.

Nebuchadnezzar then placed Zedekiah, uncle
of the recently deported Jehoiachin, on the throne
of Judah. He ruled during the next decade (597-

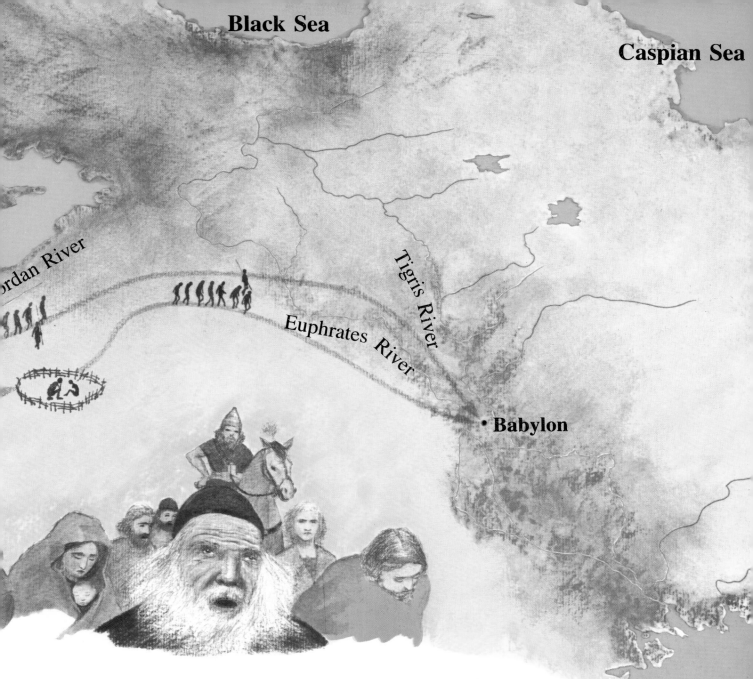

Black Sea

Caspian Sea

Jordan River

Euphrates River

Tigris River

• **Babylon**

Persian Gulf

587), but eventually he began to plot against his Babylonian overlord. Against the warnings of the prophet Jeremiah but encouraged by the Egyptians, Zedekiah declared independence from Babylonia.

Soon Nebuchadnezzar's armies swept through Judah, eventually besieging Jerusalem for eighteen months. The Temple and palace were leveled, and the city walls were torn down. In 587 B.C. Jerusalem, the city of David, was utterly destroyed. The last king of Judah, Zedekiah, was killed, and more people were deported than in 597. This time 60,000 to 80,000 people were carried off, including priests, government officials, wealthy people, deserters who had tried to escape the siege, soldiers who had been disarmed, and artisans who could perform useful work in Babylonia. All these men were deported, along with their wives and children.

Some people of Judah were left behind in the villages and countryside, especially farmers and others considered not dangerous. A member of a leading family in Judah, Gedaliah, was appointed governor over them. He established himself at Mizpah, about eight miles north of Jerusalem, and began to organize and rule for Babylonia the remnant of the Jews that remained. After some months, perhaps years, of peace under Gedaliah, however, an angry fellow countryman named Ishmael plotted with the king of Ammon to free Judah. Ishmael and other plotters murdered Gedaliah and several Babylonian soldiers with him at Mizpah.

Angered, Nebuchadnezzar once again ravaged the land and carried off hundreds more into exile. Many people of Judah fled to Egypt. The prophet Jeremiah preached in the name of God against this flight to Egypt, but fear of the Babylonians had spread too widely, and many emigrated to Egypt. They forcibly carried Jeremiah and his scribe Baruch away with them. Jeremiah never saw Judah again.

2 Exiles had to walk hundreds
of miles to Babylonia
and then were put to work.
But they were able
to keep their sense
that they were a special people.
Gradually some of the exiles
even became prosperous
in Babylonia.

The Babylonians were not as cruel toward their captives as the Assyrians were, but they did continue the Assyrian policy of deporting people from conquered territories. During the great deportation of 587 and 586, a camp for deportees was organized at Ramah, about seven miles north of Jerusalem. The suffering mass of men, women, and children, who were destined to depart for an exile from which they would not return, inspired the prophet Jeremiah to recall Rachel, the mother of Joseph and Benjamin:
"The Lord says,
'A sound is heard in Ramah,
    the sound of bitter weeping.
Rachel is crying for her children;
    they are gone,
    and she refuses to be comforted.' "
(Jeremiah 31:15 TEV)

At Ramah, donkeys, carts, tents, and provisions for the long journey were prepared. Men were tied with their elbows joined together behind their backs, or they were tied two together with their arms joined. They were lined up to march under the careful watch of armed soldiers. Women followed the carts on foot, carrying bags of food; the carts were loaded with household goods and children. The army strictly controlled the march, especially during its first days; this was to prevent the escape of possible fugitives. Once the caravan reached the edge of the desert there was no hope for any persons who fell behind, except to starve and be eaten by jackals. At that point, the men were untied and invited to cooperate in the work of the journey.

This forced march that seemed endless probably lasted several months. The route of marchers formed an arc of well over one thousand miles. They had to cross over Syria to the westernmost bend of the Euphrates; there they changed their course, heading southeast and following the great river down to the city of Babylon.

Once they had arrived at their destination, the exiles and their families were distributed among several Babylonian districts. A large number of them were employed in the construction of Babylonian temples and other public buildings. In a number of his writings Nebuchadnezzar boasted about carrying out this construction work. Many other exiles worked on maintaining the vast Babylonian network of irrigation canals on which the fertility of the soil depended. Still others found positions at the homes of the king and at the temples.

The Babylonians did not handle deported people in the same way the Assyrians had. In Babylonia the exiles were not scattered and dispersed among the existing population. They were allowed to live in distinct groups fairly close together; in this way, they were able to maintain their national and religious identity and keep up relations with other groups of their own people. Also their elders and priests were able to continue leading them.

In addition, the Babylonians did not plant new populations on evacuated lands in the way the Assyrians had; thus the territory of Judah remained more or less intact, in case the exiles returned.

During the approximately sixty years of the Babylonian Exile, conditions gradually became better for the children of Israel, especially after the death of Nebuchadnezzar in 562 B.C. Some exiles actually became wealthy in business; others began careers in Babylonian public life; still others helped maintain and organize the exiles, helping to build a spiritual community in a strange land. The exiles' rediscovery of religious faith kept alive their hope that their nation would be restored to them one day.

3 The exiles in Babylonia
mourned the destruction
of Jerusalem
and longed to return
to their homeland.

The destruction of Jerusalem and the deportation of the people to exile in Babylonia were events that deeply affected devout Jews. The Jews remembered and longed for their own country. The king, the Temple, the nation—all were gone. They especially grieved over the loss of Jerusalem, the holy city that contained the beloved Temple of God. Jewish poets and singers in exile interpreted the feelings of the people.

In Psalm 137, the author, an exile, described a scene that must have been common during the exile, especially in the early days. A group of Jewish deportees were seated on the banks of a Babylonian river, together sharing their memories of Jerusalem. Some Babylonians approached and, out of curiosity perhaps, asked about the homeland of the Jews. They asked what kinds of songs were sung there. Thus the Jews, already sad at being so far away from home, were angered by their defeat and exile. They cursed those who prevailed over them and prayed that the situation would get better. We include the text of this well-known psalm.

By the rivers of Babylon we sat down;
    there we wept when we remembered Zion.
On the willows near by
    we hung up our harps.
Those who captured us told us to sing;
    they told us to entertain them:

    "Sing us a song about Zion."

How can we sing a song to the Lord
    in a foreign land?
May I never be able to play the harp again
    if I forget you, Jerusalem!
May I never be able to sing again
    if I do not remember you,
    if I do not think of you as my greatest joy!

Remember, Lord, what the Edomites did
   the day Jerusalem was captured.
Remember how they kept saying,
   "Tear it down to the ground!"

Babylon, you will be destroyed.
Happy is the man who pays you back
   for what you have done to us —
   who takes your babies
   and smashes them against a rock.
                    (Psalm 137 TEV)

The Book of Lamentations in the Bible was thought to have been written by the prophet Jeremiah, but, in fact, it was written later. This book, too, expresses the feelings of the people about their defeat and exile. However, since it was written some time after the defeat, it is calmer in tone and includes a prayer to God to intervene and save his faithful people.

How lonely lies Jerusalem, once so full of people!
   Once honored by the world, she is now like a
      widow;
   The noblest of cities has fallen into slavery.
All night long she cries; tears run down her cheeks.

Of all her former friends, not one is left to comfort her.
   Her allies have betrayed her and are all against
   her now.

Judah's people are helpless slaves, forced away
   from home.
   They live in other lands, with no place to call
   their own —
   Surrounded by enemies, with no way to escape.
No one comes to the Temple now to worship on
   the holy days.
   The girls who sang there suffer, and the priests
   can only groan.
   The city gates stand empty, and Zion is in agony.

Her enemies succeeded; they hold her in their
   power.
   The lord has made her suffer for all her many
   sins;
   Her children have been captured and taken away.

The splendor of Jerusalem is a thing of the past.
   Her leaders are like deer that are weak from
   hunger,
   Whose strength is almost gone as they flee from
   the hunters.   (Lamentations 1:1-6 TEV)

Remember, O Lord, what has happened to us.
   Look at us, and see our disgrace.
Our property is in the hands of strangers;
   foreigners are living in our homes.
Our fathers have been killed by the enemy,
   and now our mothers are widows.
We must pay for the water we drink;
   we must buy the wood we need for fuel.
Driven hard like donkeys or camels,
   we are tired, but are allowed no rest.
To get food enough to stay alive,
   we went begging to Egypt and Assyria.
Our ancestors sinned, but now they are gone,
   and we are suffering for their sins.
We are ruled by men who are no better than slaves,
   and no one can save us from their power.
Murderers roam through the countryside;
   we risk our lives when we look for food.
                (Lamentations 5:1-9 TEV)

But you, O Lord, are king forever
   and will rule to the end of time.
Why have you abandoned us so long?
   Will you ever remember us again?
Bring us back to you, Lord! Bring us back!
   Restore our ancient glory.
Or have you rejected us forever?
   Is there no limit to your anger?
             (Lamentations 5:19-22 TEV)

4 Because the Jewish leaders
had been taken to Babylonia,
the Jews who remained
were mostly farmers
and very poor.
Like the exiles, they hoped
for a restoration
of their nation.

The Babylonians brought to their country many thousands of Jews in the deportations of 597 and 587 B.C. They took government officials, priests, artisans, and other persons who could be useful to the Babylonians and, if left in Judea, could have been the leaders of Jewish revolts against Babylonian rule. So the Jewish community was divided in two: the leadership classes, who were carried off to Babylonia, and those left behind, who were poor peasants. For the most part, the Jews who remained were farmers working the land. This is why the biblical writings produced during this period came out of the land of exile and not from the territories of the homeland.

The prophet Jeremiah noted that the Babylonians "left in Judah some of the poorest people, who owned no property, and he put them to work in the vineyards and fields" (Jeremiah 52:16 TEV). Although many thousands of the Jews were actually deported, many others remained. Of course, the Babylonians had destroyed much throughout the land, and the misery of those who remained in their homeland was great. Fortunately, however, Judah was a relatively fertile land; the cultivation of grain fields, vineyards, and olive groves could continue to produce the basic foodstuffs of the Mediterranean region. After a period of misery and deprivation, it is likely that the Jews who remained were able to work themselves back up to a more reasonable standard of living.

Judah, especially Jerusalem, continued to be extremely important to Jews everywhere. This was so even though the Temple had been destroyed

and its sacred furnishings carried away. No matter what, Jerusalem was still the center of the Jewish religion. It was the city to which the Jews hoped one day to return; there the glory of God had been manifested; according to some of the prophecies, it was in Jerusalem that the Chosen People would be finally liberated.

So Judah continued to be the Promised Land. Not only the remaining inhabitants but also the exiles loved it greatly. The Bible contains a number of writings that express the people's great love for their land. Here is one from the Book of Baruch*:

Take off the garment of your sorrow and afflic-
tion, O Jerusalem,
    and put on for ever the beauty of the glory from
    God.
Put on the robe of the righteousness from God:
    put on your head the diadem of the glory of the
    Everlasting.
For God will show your spendor everywhere un-
    der heaven.

*This passage is accepted by Roman Catholics but not by most Protestants.

For your name will for ever be called by God,
    "Peace of righteousness and glory of godliness."
Arise, O Jerusalem, stand upon the height
    and look toward the east,
and see your children gathered from west and east,
    at the word of the Holy One,
    rejoicing that God has remembered them.
For they went forth from you on foot,
    led away by their enemies;
but God will bring them back to you,
    carried in glory, as on a royal throne.
For God has ordered that every high mountain and
        the everlasting hills be made low
    and the valleys filled up, to make level ground,
    so that Israel may walk safely in the glory of
    God.
The woods and every fragrant tree
    have shaded Israel at God's command.
For God will lead Israel with joy,
    in the light of his glory,
    with the mercy and righteousness that come from
    him.   (Baruch 5:1-9)

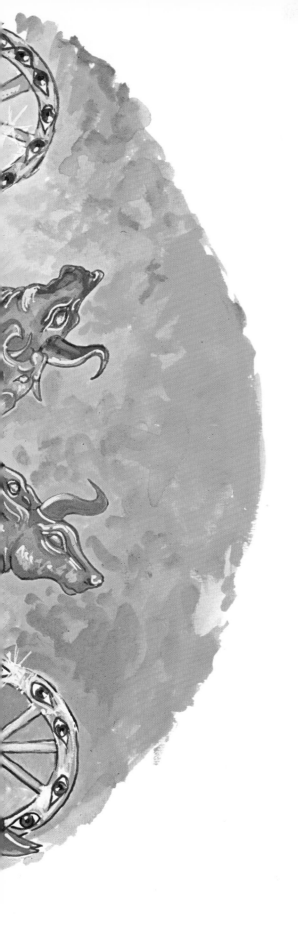

5 The Book of Ezekiel
records the prophet's
message of hope
to the other exiles:
God had not abandoned them
but was still with them,
even in Babylonia.

Among the exiles deported in 597 B.C. there was a priest
whose name was Ezekiel. When he had been in Babylonia for five years, assigned to help maintain a Babylonian irrigation canal, he had an extraordinary vision.

In it, a wild wind swept down from the north towards
the prophet, carrying with it a cloud of fire. In the center
of this fiery cloud of light, Ezekiel could make out the
likenesses of four strange living creatures. Each of the
four had the face of a human, eagles' wings, and bodies
that were partly those of bulls and partly those of lions.
They resembled the Assyro-Babylonian cherubim, winged
creatures whose statues were often placed at the en-
trances of important buildings. In the midst of these
creatures the prophet saw burning coals that resembled
torches. The coals were the fire of God; the creatures
served God and represented the service all creatures owe
God.

At the side of each creature there was a wheel with
eyes set into its rims; each wheel moved in the direction
set by the darting creatures. All four wheels formed a
kind of chariot of fire that moved from north to south.

Then the prophet Ezekiel heard a voice from above.
The four creatures stopped moving. Ezekiel saw a vision
of God sitting on the divine throne, covered with a man-
tle of flame. When the prophet saw God, he, like Isaiah
before him, threw himself down before the glory of God.

Then a voice spoke to him and told him to rise. "Mortal man, stand up . . . I am sending you to the people
of Israel. They have rebelled and turned against me
and are still rebels, just as their ancestors were. They
are stubborn and do not respect me, so I am sending
you to tell them what I, the Sovereign Lord, am saying to them. Whether those rebels listen to you or not,
they will know that a prophet has been among them."
(Ezekiel 2:1, 3-5 TEV)

This is the way in which Ezekiel was given his mission as a prophet. The message received by Ezekiel indicated that the people in exile had not been abandoned
by God. By coming from the north, the chariot of fire
had traveled the same route the exiles had taken.

So God was not present only in Jerusalem. God had
followed his people into exile, and the prophet was there
to give witness to God's divine presence to anyone who
doubted. Nobody had to despair just because it was no
longer possible to go to Jerusalem. God was present in
Babylonia—and it was necessary to follow God's holy
will there, to be sorry for past sins, and to worship God
sincerely.

6 Ezekiel promised that God
would renew his chosen people.
He also spoke about
personal responsibility.
No longer would persons suffer
for the sins of their parents.

Biblical scholars point out two distinct periods in
the prophetic work of Ezekiel. The first period
extended from 593 B.C., the year of his call by
God, to 587, the year of the fall of Jerusalem. The
second period extended from 587 until around 571,
the probable year of the prophet's death.

Not only were these two periods different in
length, but they were also rather different in the
content of Ezekiel's preaching. During the first
period, Ezekiel took up Jeremiah's familiar theme,
scolding his fellow Jews for imagining that they
would soon be able to return from their exile. God
was present in Babylonia. Israel had been delivered into the hands of the conqueror, who was
God's instrument for punishment. Rebellion against
God was useless; it would only cause a more terrible punishment still.

During the second period of his preaching,
however, the prophet realized that he needed to
hearten and encourage the people. While it was
true that deliverance from the Babylonians would
not happen soon, nevertheless, God's punishment
was not meant to destroy. It was meant to bring
about a renewal of the covenant. God would personally lead the people, since their leaders had
proved incapable of leading them. When that happened, there would be a new Temple, new worship, and new settlement in the Promised Land.
At the same time, God would punish the people's
oppressor, whom he had temporarily permitted to
act as an instrument of punishment and purification.

One of Ezekiel's favorite themes as a prophet was that of personal responsibility. Children did not have to suffer for the sins of their fathers and mothers. Even though the older generation might have abandoned the light and the glory of God and adopted idol worship, their children could turn away from those sins and return to the light. They did not have to pay, as had once been said, for the sins of their fathers and mothers. God was just and would judge persons according to what they themselves deserved.

Here are some of the actual words of the prophet Ezekiel:

"But you took advantage of your beauty and fame to sleep with everyone who came along. You used some of your clothes to decorate your places of worship, and just like a prostitute, you gave yourself to everyone. You took the silver and gold jewelry that I had given you, used it to make male images, and committed adultery with them. You took the embroidered clothes I gave you and put them on the images, and you offered to the images the olive oil and incense I had given you. I gave you food—the best flour, olive oil, and honey—but you offered it as a sacrifice to win the favor of idols." This is what the Sovereign Lord says.

(Ezekiel 16:15-19 TEV)

The Lord spoke to me and said, "What is this proverb people keep repeating in the land of Israel?

'The parents ate the sour grapes,
But the children got the sour taste.'

"As surely as I am the living God," says the Sovereign Lord, "you will not repeat this proverb in Israel any more. The life of every person belongs to me, the life of the parent as well as that of the child. The person who sins is the one who will die.

"Suppose there is a truly good man, righteous and honest. He doesn't worship the idols of the Israelites or eat the sacrifices offered at forbidden shrines. He doesn't seduce another man's wife or have intercourse with a woman during her period. He doesn't cheat or rob anyone. He returns what a borrower gives him as security; he feeds the hungry and gives clothing to the naked. He doesn't lend money for profit. He refuses to do evil and gives an honest decision in any dispute. Such a man obeys my commands and carefully keeps my laws. He is righteous, and he will live," says the Sovereign Lord. (Ezekiel 18:1-9 TEV)

7 Ezekiel had a vision of a desert
full of dry bones
that came to life.
This vision was a promise
that God's people would
return to their homeland.

God explained the meaning of this strange vision. The dry bones represented the exiled Jews who, deaf to the voice of God, had lost all hope of rebirth. Although the people were as good as dead, God himself had the power to bring them back to life and lead them back to their homeland. Although Ezekiel did not interpret his vision to mean that the dead would be resurrected, his vision did draw the attention of the Jews to the possibility of life after death.

One of Ezekiel's most famous prophecies was the one about the dry bones that returned to life. Inspired by the spirit of God, Ezekiel had a vision of a valley of dry bones, where he saw an enormous number of bones rise up and put themselves together into bodies and return to life.

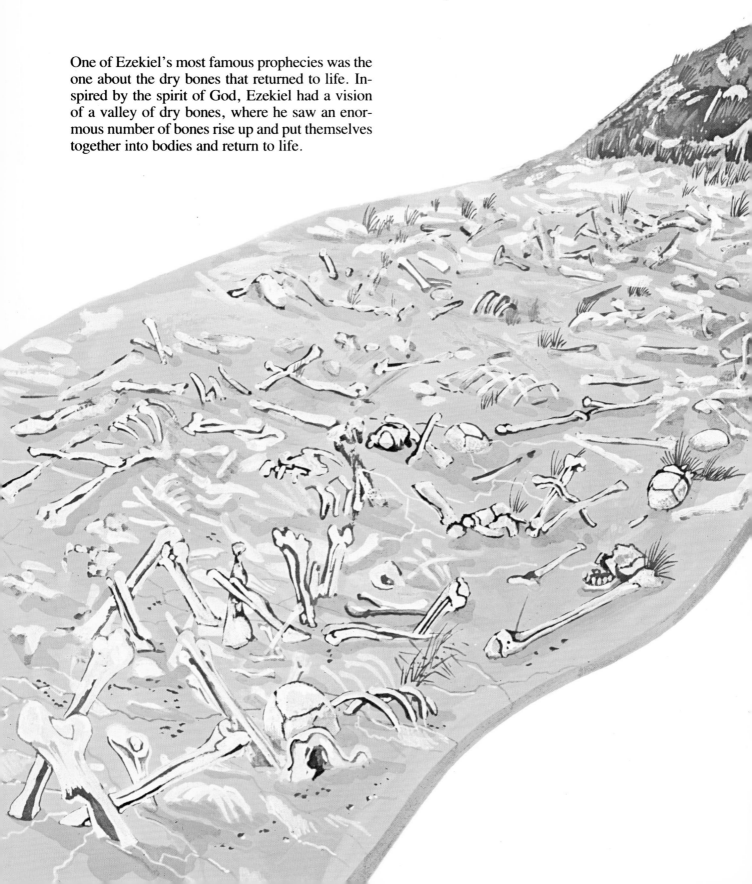

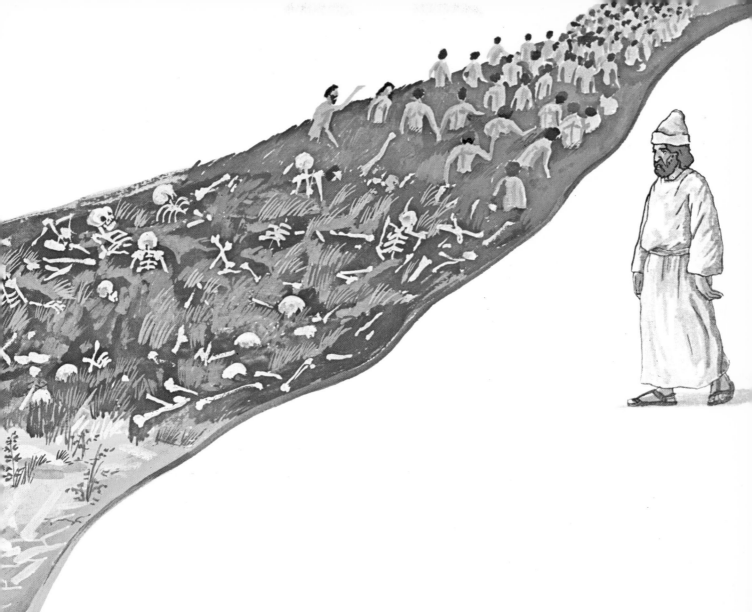

I felt the powerful presence of the Lord, and his spirit took me and set me down in a valley where the ground was covered with bones. He led me all around the valley, and I could see that there were very many bones and that they were very dry. He said to me, "Mortal man, can these bones come back to life?"

I replied, "Sovereign Lord, only you can answer that!"

He said, "Prophesy to the bones. Tell these dry bones to listen to the word of the Lord. Tell them that I, the Sovereign Lord, am saying to them: I am going to put breath into you and bring you back to life. I will give you sinews and muscles, and cover you with skin. I will put breath into you and bring you back to life. Then you will know that I am the Lord."

So I prophesied as I had been told. While I was speaking, I heard a rattling noise, and the bones began to join together. While I watched, the bones were covered with sinews and muscles, and then with skin. But there was no breath in the bodies.

God said to me, "Mortal man, prophesy to the wind. Tell the wind that the Sovereign Lord commands it to come from every direction, to breathe into these dead bodies, and to bring them back to life."

So I prophesied as I had been told. Breath entered the bodies, and they came to life and stood up. There were enough of them to form an army.

God said to me, "Mortal man, the people of Israel are like these bones. They say that they are dried up, without any hope and with no future. So prophesy to my people Israel and tell them that I, the Lord God, am going to open their graves. I am going to take them out and bring them back to the land of Israel. When I open the graves where my people are buried and bring them out, they will know that I am the Lord. I will put my breath in them, bring them back to life, and let them live in their own land. Then they will know that I am the Lord. I have promised that I would do this—and I will. I, the Lord, have spoken."

(Ezekiel 37:1-14 TEV)

8 Ezekiel had visions
of a splendid new temple,
priests and people
faithful to God,
and a society of prosperity
and social justice.

The Book of Ezekiel ends with a series of visions that describe the life of the People of God after they returned to the Promised Land. There the people would turn from sin and honor the covenant made by Moses. God would cleanse the people and give them new help in understanding and loving his Law.

"I will give you a new heart and a new mind. I will take away your stubborn heart of stone and give you an obedient heart. I will put my spirit in you and will see to it that you follow my laws and keep all the commands I have given you. Then you will live in the land I gave your ancestors. You will be my people, and I will be your God."   (Ezekiel 36:26-28 TEV)

In another vision, Ezekiel saw a future in which Israel and Judah would be reunited and governed by a king of David's line. He saw Mount Zion in Jerusalem, where a new Temple was to be constructed. Then an extraordinary being, a bronze angel, revealed to the prophet the exact dimensions of the new Temple; these dimensions were approximately the same as those of the old Temple destroyed by the Babylonians. The Temple's sacred furnishings, however, would be more rich and splendid than before and would be purified of any pagan influences for the worship of the true God. This worship required holiness and, for that reason, also required the new heart and the new spirit that God would give the faithful.

Even the ministers of religion needed to be purified. Ezekiel divided religious leaders into three classes: priests, Levites, and leaders of the people. The priests were to be the preexilic priests who had remained faithful; they were called the Zadokites, or "sons of Zadok." (Ezekiel himself belonged to this class.) However, so that the priests could not profit from their privileged position, they were not to be allowed to own land; they would have to live on the offerings of the faithful.

By the side of the Zadokites would be the Levites. They would assist the priests in religious ceremonies. The leaders of the people would no longer be allowed to exercise any religious functions; they would be given the task of redistributing the land among the various tribes.

After having described the new Temple and those who would serve its altar, Ezekiel saw a vision of a stream welling up from under the Temple and flowing east, making the waters of the Dead Sea fresh and producing good crops in all the lands around it. With this new fertility of the land, it would have been possible to divide up the good land equally among all the tribes. In this way, the prophet Ezekiel showed a new concern for equality and social justice among the people.

9 The Exile led Jews to collect the writings we know as the Old Testament. These writings helped them keep their identity and remember their special relationship to the one God.

The preaching of the prophet Ezekiel was set down in writing and carefully preserved by his disciples. Ezekiel's preaching made the Jews ask themselves some questions about just who they were as a people. The fact that they were living in exile stirred up even more questions about their identity. Why were they so different from other peoples? Why was their God, Yahweh, not like the gods of the Babylonians? Why had Yahweh not saved them? Why were they in exile? Did their God rule over the land where they now found themselves? Could their God not help them? Were they abandoned forever, or was there still some hope for them?

This was the first time these questions had been asked so directly and forcefully. Attempts to answer them were not in Ezekiel alone; earlier prophetic books also had tried to give answers. The scribes of the court in Judah and the exiled priests had saved from destruction some of these books, written on scrolls of papyrus or leather, and they had brought these books with them as precious keepsakes from their homeland. There were the writings of the prophets Amos and Hosea, who had foretold the destruction of the kingdom of Israel as a punishment of God. There were the writings of Micah and Isaiah, who scolded the people for their sins but also extended hope and wonderful promises. There were other prophetic writings as well, including the very recent prophecies of Jeremiah and some prophecies written down by Baruch. Taken all together, these writings criticized the people for their behavior but also provided some answers to the questions of the exile. The writings said to the people, "God has not abandoned you; you have abandoned God. God still wants to save you; he is merely waiting for you to return to him."

At the same time that the prophetic writings were being preserved and transcribed by scribes in exile, the conquests of Cyrus the Persian were bringing some real changes in the world's political situation and in the situation of the exiles. Then a new prophet among the exiles in Babylon wrote

what is sometimes called the "book of consolations." These writings became part (chapters 40-55) of the Book of Isaiah, as we know it in the Bible. This prophet foretold the return to Jerusalem and a new beginning for a Jewish nation renewed in its faith in a savior-God.

The Book of Deuteronomy, which had served as the basis for Josiah's reforms, linked the Israelites' existence as a nation in the Promised Land with their faithfulness to the covenant with God. Deuteronomy expressed this link through alternate blessings and curses on the people, depending upon their conduct.

Using the ideas in Deuteronomy, a writer (or group of writers) whom we call "the deuteronomist" collected all the ancient writings about the conquest of the Promised Land and about the periods of the judges and kings. These writings showed that the Exile happened neither through blind fate nor through the superiority of the pagans and their gods. Like all the Israelites' misfortunes, the Exile was something that came about because the people practiced pagan idolatry. The books of Joshua, Judges, Samuel and Kings were gathered together at this time in order to illustrate this theme.

The Pentateuch, the first five books of the Bible, also achieved its final form about this time. These ancient documents that centered on Moses and the covenant of Sinai also included material on the promise made to Abraham and the patriarchs. They showed that the people who came out of Egypt were the descendants of Abraham. To these ancient narratives and genealogies were added codes of laws and religious practices, especially those associated in some way with Moses. Finally, an account of the Creation was included.

During this time period the Jews definitely left behind pagan superstitions. The theme constantly repeated by the prophets became accepted universally among the Jews, even among the ordinary people: There is one unique God, Yahweh, who is the true God, the Creator of the universe. There are no other gods.

10 Second Isaiah told how
Cyrus of Persia was part of God's plans.
He prophesied about
a servant of God, whose suffering
would bring forgiveness and salvation.

As mentioned in the previous chapter, a major new prophet appeared during the Exile between about 550 and 540 B.C. His book is sometimes called "the book of consolations" because his prophecies comforted, or consoled, the people. It was added to the Book of Isaiah without any indication that it was by a different author or that it was written at a later time. Modern Bible scholars have established that chapters 40 to 55 of the Book of Isaiah are the work of this anonymous prophet whom they call "Second Isaiah."

This prophet's message includes hope, consolation, advice, and encouragement for the exiled people. Second Isaiah lived at a time of national defeat and disaster, just as Jeremiah and Ezekiel had. However, the situation had changed somewhat. By now the Babylonians, who had defeated the kingdom of Judah and carried off its inhabitants into exile, were themselves going into decline. The prophet wrote about the rising star of a king who would defeat the Babylonians and allow the Jews to return to their homeland. These prophecies were about Cyrus the Persian.

However, it was not Cyrus' successes and victories themselves that most interested Second Isaiah. Rather, he saw Cyrus as an instrument of justice in the hands of God. Not only would Cyrus permit the Jews to return to their homeland, but Cyrus himself would accept the God of Israel and spread his worship through the world. With Second Isaiah, the Jews came face to face with the idea of a universal God. God was seen not only as the Lord of Judah, a small and insignificant province in the Babylonian Empire; God was also seen as the Lord of history, who moved and governed the peoples of all the world according to divine plan.

Even in this vision of a universal God, Jerusalem was to remain the center of the worship of the one true God, and the Chosen People of God had a worldwide mission to represent the cause of God in the world.

Second Isaiah prophesied about the appearance of a mysterious representative of God on the earth, to be known as "the servant of Yahweh." A lover of justice and peace, this servant would be the hope of the people, and even kings would heed him. At the same time, the servant would suffer greatly for the sins of humanity, but after his torments he would triumph, and his sufferings would be the salvation of all people.

Much later, the Christian Church considered these servant prophecies to refer to Jesus the Christ, whose suffering and death, followed by resurrection from the dead, saved the world.

"It was the will of the Lord that his servant
    grow like a plant taking root in dry ground.
He had no dignity or beauty
    to make us take notice of him.
There was nothing attractive about him,
    nothing that would draw us to him.

"But he endured the suffering that should have
        been ours,
    the pain that we should have borne.
All the while we thought that his suffering
    was punishment sent by God.
But because of our sins he was wounded,
    beaten because of the evil we did.
We are healed by the punishment he suffered,
    made whole by the blows he received.
All of us were like sheep that were lost,
    each of us going his own way.
But the Lord made the punishment fall on him,
    the punishment all of us deserved."

The Lord says,
"It was my will that he should suffer;
    his death was a sacrifice to bring forgiveness.
And so he will see his descendants;
    he will live a long life,
    and through him my purpose will succeed.
After a life of suffering, he will again have joy;
    he will know that he did not suffer in vain.
My devoted servant, with whom I am pleased,
    will bear the punishment of many
    and for his sake I will forgive them.
And so I will give him a place of honor,
    a place among great and powerful men.
He willingly gave his life
    and shared the fate of evil men.
He took the place of many sinners
    and prayed that they might be forgiven."
                    (Isaiah 53:2, 4-6, 10-12 TEV)

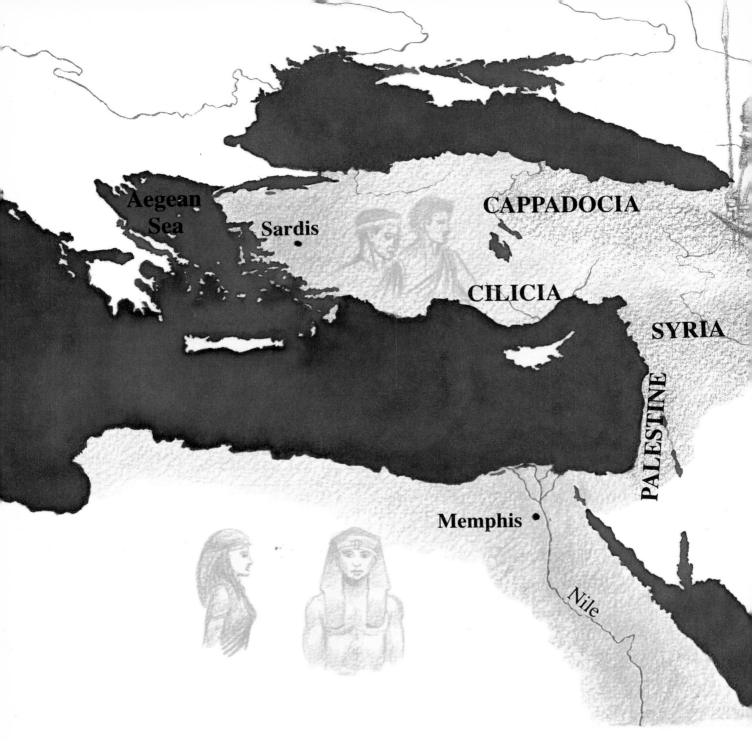

11 After conquering Judah in 587 B.C., Babylonia declined rapidly in power, and Persia under Cyrus became the most powerful nation around Palestine.

In 612 B.C. Nineveh (Assyria) fell to Nabopolassar, king of Babylonia, and Cyaxares, king of Media. Shortly after, in 605 B.C., the Babylonians defeated Pharaoh Neco of Egypt, who had invaded Syria and Palestine. Then for some years the empires in the ancient Near East remained stable. This peaceful state of affairs was further helped along in 585 B.C. when the kingdom of Media and the kingdom of Lydia agreed to divide up their rule over Asia Minor.

Thus the rule of the ancient Medes extended from present-day Iran to Cappadocia, in present-day Turkey; its southern frontier bordered on the territory of the Babylonians. The Babylonian Empire included Cilicia, Phoenicia, Palestine, and Syria and extended down the Tigris and Euphrates rivers to the Persian Gulf.

So long as Nebuchadnezzar lived, Babylonia was very powerful. In 574 B.C., after a thirteen-year siege, Babylonia took the city of Tyre, which had been considered almost impossible to conquer since it was built on a little island off the coast. In 568-67 B.C. Nebuchadnezzar invaded Egypt, with serious consequences for the Jews who earlier had taken refuge there.

After the death of Nebuchadnezzar in 562 B.C., however, the decline of Babylonia was quite rapid.

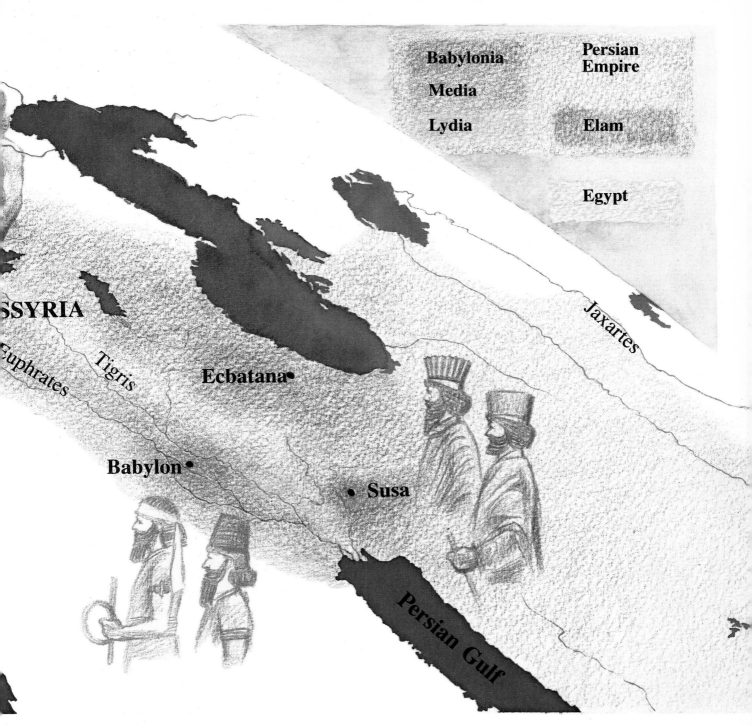

The last Babylonian sovereign, Nabonidus (556-539), stirred up great discontent among his subjects by his religious policies. Among other things, he ordered that all the statues and idols of the gods worshiped among all the peoples subject to him should be brought to Babylon. He was interested in history and archeology and in digging up old documents and inscriptions from the earlier times of the Sumerians and the Akkadians. But he had no skill as a military leader.

As Babylonia declined, the power of the Persians under Cyrus grew. Originally Cyrus was under the rule of Astyages, son of Cyaxares, king of Media. (According to Greek historians, Cyrus was the son of one of Astyages' daughters.) From his capital at Ecbatana (Hamadan), Astyages ruled directly over only a number of territories south of Media. Cyrus, one of those subject to him, was the king of Anzan, the region around Susa that the

Babylonians called Elam. He dedicated himself to uniting the southern tribes of the region in a new and powerful kingdom named Persia. In 553 B.C. he was strong enough to march against Astyages himself. By 550 B.C. Cyrus had conquered the capital, Ecbatana, and he became king of the Medes and the Persians. Contrary to the custom of the times, Cyrus did not allow Ecbatana to be sacked; he spared the city and continued to honor Astyages after his defeat.

Croesus, the last king of Lydia, famous in history for his wealth, resisted the invation of Cyrus. However, Croesus was defeated at Sardis in 546 B.C. The Persian empire now extended all the way west to the Aegean Sea. In 540 B.C. Cyrus established the eastern borders of his empire on the Jaxartes (Syr Darya). At that point he was ready to turn his attention towards the Babylonian Empire.

12 In 539 B.C. Cyrus conquered Babylon and became ruler of an immense empire. Cyrus was more generous than Babylonian rulers toward conquered peoples and their religions.

The speed of the conquests made by Cyrus, the word of his generosity towards the conquered, and his respect for the religions of subject peoples not only excited the peoples who were restless under Babylonian rule; it also was welcome news to the Babylonians themselves, for they had been infuriated by the religious policies of Nabonidus.

Cyrus tried to profit from that situation. From 545 B.C. on, in fact, he even had a Babylonian ally in Gobryas, governor of Gutium, the region east of the Tigris. By this time, Nabonidus had returned from his voluntary exile in the Arabian desert and had begun to prepare himself for the worst. In the autumn of 539 B.C. Cyrus won his first victory over the Babylonians at Opis on the Tigris; this victory opened up the road to Babylon. Two weeks later the Babylonians clashed with troops commanded directly by Nabonidus at Sippar, not far from Babylon. Meanwhile, Gobryas, the Babylonian ally of Cyrus, moved directly on the capital.

Nabonidus was defeated and forced to flee; he was later captured but his life was spared. Two days after the victory of Cyrus at Sippar, Gobryas entered Babylon, apparently without any opposition. The troops of the conquering armies were themselves assigned to guard the temples to ensure that there would be no plundering or sacking.

When Cyrus entered the capital to take possession of the entire Babylonian realm, he was greeted like a liberator, not like a conqueror. He guaranteed the safety of the city and decreed an end to the fighting.

Later the Greek historian Herodotus handed down a famous legend about Cyrus' conquest of Babylon. According to Herodotus, Cyrus arranged to change the course of the Euphrates, the river which ran through the city. Then the Persian army, marching through the dry riverbed, entered the city by surprise while the Babylonians were celebrating a feast. The reality probably is that the besieged themselves opened the gates of the city to the Persians. The Babylonian chronicle of Nabonidus provides dates for these successive events too close together to permit such a long and complex operation as changing the course of the Euphrates.

Cyrus had become the ruler of an immense empire. The discontent of the conquered peoples subject to Babylonia had helped him make his conquests. Both out of the desire to reward his supporters and by his natural tendencies, he began a policy of dispersing what the Babylonians had tried to concentrate in Babylon. One of the first problems he faced was the statues and idols of the subject peoples. Cyrus was probably himself a Zoroastrian in religion, but in his official policy he was respectful of the divinities of all his subject peoples, beginning with Marduk, the main god of Babylonia. The statues of other divinities of subject peoples, which had been brought to Babylon by Nabonidus were all triumphantly returned to their original places.

But not only the statutes were returned. Under this new policy, whole peoples who had been exiled were allowed and even helped to return to their original homelands and to rebuild their abandoned temples and sanctuaries. The new ruler made himself available to representatives of the displaced populations in order to learn of their wishes and to help them carry them out. Naturally Cyrus' policy applied to the exiles from the kingdom of Judah and to the furnishings from the Temple in Jerusalem.

13 The Edict of Cyrus allowed
the Jews and other exiles
to return
to their own homelands.

Having spared conquered Babylon from both massacre and plunder, Cyrus wanted to show that his policy was one of liberty, in contrast to the policies followed by Nebuchadnezzar and his successors in the Babylonian empire. Did the Babylonians deport entire peoples and carry them off into exile? Very well, now Cyrus would allow them to return and rebuild their national life (always under the rule of the king of Persia, of course). Did the Babylonians even bring to Babylon all the statues and furnishings of the temples of conquered peoples? Very well, now they could be returned to their respective cities and sanctuaries.

All these declarations of Cyrus the Great were known as "the Edict of Cyrus"; they were recorded in a document known as "the Cylinder of Cyrus." The "cylinder" in question was made out of clay; a long description of the conquests of Cyrus and the beginning of his reign at Babylon were inscribed on this cylinder in cuneiform characters (wedge-shaped letters). After this edict was issued in 538 B.C., caravans of people were organized to return to their original homes, carrying with them their families, household goods, and the statues of their gods. There was new hope for a better, freer life.

Cyrus was probably a monotheist (believer in one God), or something very close to it. In the Zoroastrian religion which he practiced, Ahura-Mazda, "the wise Lord," was believed to be opposed to the spirit of evil. For political reasons,

however, Cyrus had to represent himself as the one who executed the will of Marduk, the god of the Babylonians, or of the respective gods of the peoples over whom he ruled. Perhaps in his mind he identified all these gods with Ahura-Mazda.

It must have been easy for Cyrus to identify the divine being he worshiped with the one God worshiped by his Jewish subjects; this God could not be represented by statues and images. For this reason the Edict of Cyrus as it applied to the Jews was worded in an interesting fashion:

"This is the command of Cyrus, Emperor of Persia. The Lord, the God of Heaven, has made me ruler over the whole world and has given me the responsibility of building a temple for him in Jerusalem in Judah. May God be with all of you who are his people. You are to go to Jerusalem and rebuild the Temple of the Lord, the God of Israel, the God who is worshiped in Jerusalem. If any of his people in exile need help to return, their neighbors are to give them this help. They are to provide them with silver and gold, supplies and pack animals, as well as offerings to present in the Temple of God in Jerusalem."   (Ezra 1:2-4 TEV)

An echo of the joy which the Edict of Cyrus caused among the exiled Jews can be heard in Psalm 126, which compared the return of the exiles with the return of the winter rains to the arid Negeb desert south of the kingdom of Judah:

When the Lord restored the fortunes of Zion,
    we were like those who dream.
Then our mouth was filled with laughter,
    and our tongue with shouts of joy;
then they said among the nations,
    "The Lord has done great things for them."
The Lord has done great things for us;
    we are glad.
Restore our fortunes, O Lord,
    like the watercourses in the Negeb!
May those who sow in tears
    reap with shouts of joy!
He that goes forth weeping,
    bearing the seed for sowing,
shall come home with shouts of joy,
    bringing his sheaves with him.
                                    (Psalm 126)

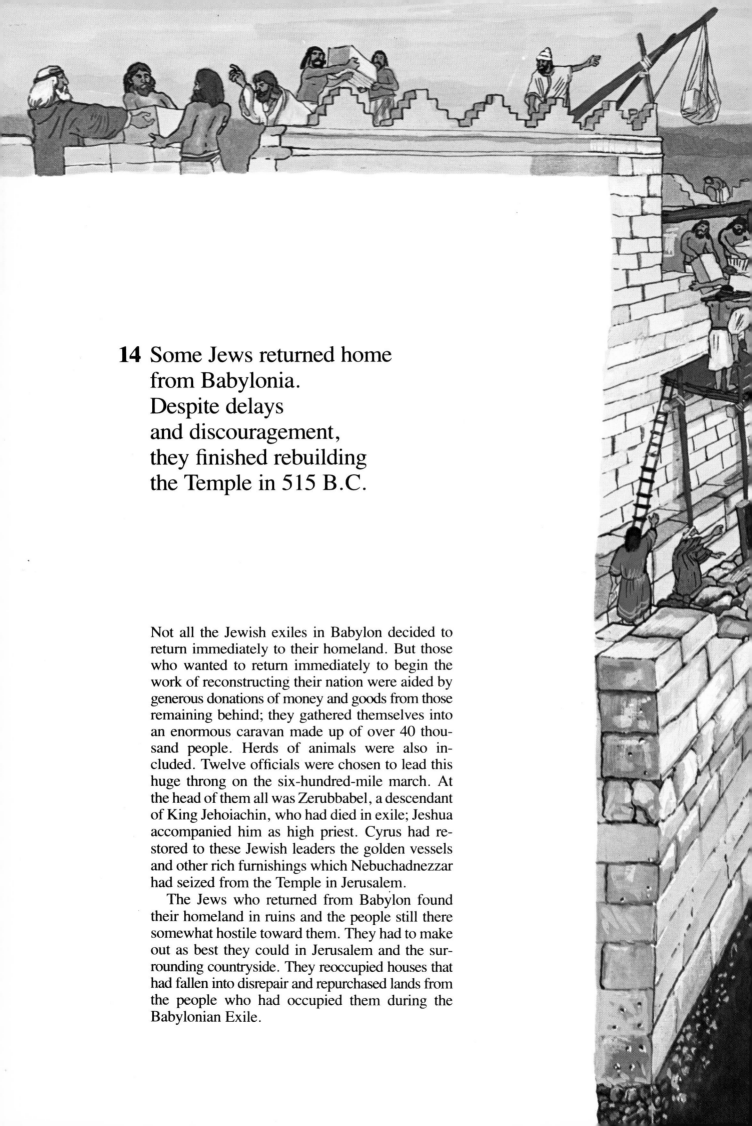

14 Some Jews returned home
from Babylonia.
Despite delays
and discouragement,
they finished rebuilding
the Temple in 515 B.C.

Not all the Jewish exiles in Babylon decided to
return immediately to their homeland. But those
who wanted to return immediately to begin the
work of reconstructing their nation were aided by
generous donations of money and goods from those
remaining behind; they gathered themselves into
an enormous caravan made up of over 40 thousand people. Herds of animals were also included. Twelve officials were chosen to lead this
huge throng on the six-hundred-mile march. At
the head of them all was Zerubbabel, a descendant
of King Jehoiachin, who had died in exile; Jeshua
accompanied him as high priest. Cyrus had restored to these Jewish leaders the golden vessels
and other rich furnishings which Nebuchadnezzar
had seized from the Temple in Jerusalem.

The Jews who returned from Babylon found
their homeland in ruins and the people still there
somewhat hostile toward them. They had to make
out as best they could in Jerusalem and the surrounding countryside. They reoccupied houses that
had fallen into disrepair and repurchased lands from
the people who had occupied them during the
Babylonian Exile.

One of the very first thoughts of the returning exiles was to rebuild the Altar of Holocausts so that the offering of sacrifice to Yahweh could begin again. The rebuilding of the Temple, however, which was begun the year after the arrival of the exiles, proved to be a lengthy task. For one thing, the Samaritans were hostile to the project; they had at first offered to participate in the rebuilding of the Temple, but the Jews had refused. The Jews were concerned with their own racial identity; they demanded clear proof of descent from the Hebrew tribes and did not want to be involved with the Samaritans, who were of mixed race. The Jews also considered that the Samaritans had contaminated the worship of Yahweh by pagan practices.

The rejected Samaritans, along with other non-Jewish inhabitants who were unhappy to see the returned exiles, therefore, began actively opposing the rebuilding of the Temple. Progress was very slow, and, in fact, work on it stopped altogether for almost fifteen years.

Meanwhile, Cambyses (530-522 B.C.) succeeded his father Cyrus on the throne of Persia, and Cambyses was in turn succeeded by Darius (521-486 B.C.). One day in the second year of Darius' reign, when Zerubbabel and the high priest Jeshua were gathered around the altar with other faithful Jews, a new prophet appeared on the scene. His name was Haggai, and he rebuked the people for living in comfortable houses of their own while neglecting to rebuild the Temple for the worship of God. As a result of Haggai's words, work was resumed in the year 520 B.C. and went on for some four years.

Still another prophet, Zechariah, also began to encourage the builders to carry on. The Samaritans appealed to higher authorities in the Empire to try to block the work. However, the Edict of Cyrus was located in the records of the Persian Empire. Darius renewed it, and he threatened punishment to anyone who tried to stop the work.

The new Temple was built with the same dimensions and style as Solomon's, but the quality of construction and the materials used were much poorer. Some of the older Jews wept because the rebuilt Temple was not nearly as magnificent as the one they remembered from their youth. But the prophet Haggai declared that the new Temple would be more glorious than the old because the age of a Messiah would begin during its lifetime.

The new Temple was rededicated in 515 B.C., and the first Passover celebrations took place in it. Some of the people of the old northern kingdom of Israel who had remained faithful to the God of their fathers and mothers took part in these solemn celebrations.

15 The prophets Zechariah and Haggai encouraged those rebuilding the Temple. Malachi warned of punishment for those who neglected the worship of God.

The prophets Haggai and Zechariah, then, played a significant role in Jewish history by their encouraging those rebuilding the Temple. For Haggai, who preached solely during the year 520 B.C., the difficulties which the returned exiles encountered were due to the failure of the people to rebuild the Temple. According to him, the time of salvation would begin only when the house of God was completed and the official worship of God resumed.

The prophet Zechariah began his mission just a few months after Haggai. After a series of eight visions, he confirmed the predictions of Haggai. He emphasized the coming of the messianic era, when humankind would be saved. He also spoke of the role of priests in a new covenant.

The activity of these two prophets, called "the prophets of the Temple," was limited both in the time they preached and in the themes of their preaching. However, their importance in the history of salvation should not be undervalued. They both understood that faith in God cannot be indefinitely kept alive without some definite outward and visible sign and some specific place where God is regularly worshiped. And indeed for all Jews after that time, whether in Palestine or in Jewish communities elsewhere, the Temple in Jerusalem was the place of hope that continued to guarantee the presence of God among his people.

The Book of Malachi is the last book in the Old Testament. Like Second Isaiah, this book probably collects a number of anonymous prophecies. In fact, Malachi is not a name, but a Hebrew word meaning "my messenger." We know nothing of the life of this prophet, if indeed he was a specific, single prophet. From a careful study of the book it is possible to conclude that these prophecies were delivered sometime between the year 515 B.C., the date of the consecration of the Temple, and 445 B.C., the dates of the reforms of Nehemiah. The Book of Malachi shows a prophet who was more discouraged than were Haggai and Zechariah. The spirits of the Jewish settlers in and around Jerusalem were at a low ebb, partly due to lean harvests and drought and partly because Judea remained only an obscure corner of the Persian Empire.

The preaching of Malachi had a threatening tone: the punishment was surely coming to those who ignored God. Two kinds of persons in particular were testing God: priests who neglected their duties in regard to official worship, and Jews who divorced their Jewish wives and married foreigners. After so many efforts at reform had been made, the prophet thought the situation was desperate. He thought only the coming of the Messiah could really remedy things; only the Messiah would purify the worship of God, bring low the proud, and raise up the poor, workers, widows, and orphans.

To finish this brief look at some of the last prophetic books of the Hebrew Bible, we will read a little chapter that was added to the Book of Zechariah. Scholars think that just as there was a Second Isaiah, so there was a "Second Zechariah." This anonymous prophet carried on his work some time after Haggai and Zechariah, towards the end of the fourth century B.C., after Palestine had already been occupied by Alexander the Great. This Second Zechariah's writing proved to be especially important for its idea of a Messiah, a savior. He described some of the traits of the true Messiah, and some of these were later picked up by the gospel writers. According to Second Zechariah, the coming of the Messiah would be peaceful; Jerusalem would be purified and her enemies defeated and sent away; and people from all over the world would come to Jerusalem to worship the true God:

On that day there shall be neither cold nor frost. And there shall be continuous day (it is known to the Lord), not day and not night, for at evening time there shall be light.

On that day living waters shall flow out from Jerusalem, half of them to the eastern sea and half of them to the western sea; it shall continue in summer as in winter.

And the Lord will become king over all the earth; on that day the Lord will be one and his name one.

The whole land shall be turned into a plain from Geba to Rimmon south of Jerusalem. But Jerusalem shall remain aloft upon its site from the Gate of Benjamin to the place of the former gate, to the Corner Gate, and from the Tower of Hananel to the king's wine presses. And it shall be inhabited, for there shall be no more curse; Jerusalem shall dwell in security.

(Zechariah 14:6-11)

16 Third Isaiah described the future glory of Jerusalem, which all peoples of the world would see.

In the tenth chapter of this book, we studied Second Isaiah, an anonymous prophet in Babylon whose preachings are contained in chapters 40-55 of the Book of Isaiah. This prophet had foretold the return of the exiles and had regarded Cyrus the Great as the king who would save the Jews and help spread the worship of the true God throughout the world. These prophecies were proven true only in part. The Jews indeed returned from exile, but Cyrus was not converted to the worship of Yahweh; nor was the life of the returned exiles as glorious as the prophet had predicted.

Biblical scholars have identified a "Third Isaiah," a Jew who had returned to Judah. From about the year 520 B.C. he added to the work of the First and Second Isaiahs. His prophecies are contained in the last chapters (56-66) of the Book of Isaiah; they were added to that particular book because they resemble Second Isaiah in both style and content.

The message of this anonymous prophet is as follows: If God's promises have not come about, the fault lies neither in God nor in the prophets, but rather in the people, who failed to be converted in their hearts to God. So long as injustices persisted and God was not worshiped with a pure heart, then the expected appearance of God would not happen. If the people would be converted, however, God would reveal himself; Jerusalem would become the center of the world and all the peoples of the earth would flock there. This theme of a revelation of God, after which all the peoples of the earth would recognize his rule, also appears in some of the psalms.

These passages from Third Isaiah poetically describe with rich images the flocking of people into the holy city to take part in the joy and glory of those chosen:

Arise, Jerusalem, and shine like the sun;
The glory of the Lord is shining on you!
Other nations will be covered by darkness,

But on you the light of the Lord will shine;
The brightness of his presence will be with you.
Nations will be drawn to your light,
And kings to the dawning of your new day.

Look around you and see what is happening:
Your people are gathering to come home!
Your sons will come from far away;
Your daughters will be carried like children.
You will see this and be filled with joy;
You will tremble with excitement.
The wealth of the nations will be brought to
   you;
From across the sea their riches will come.

Great caravans of camels will come, from Mi-
   dian and Ephah.
They will come from Sheba, bringing gold and
   incense.
People will tell the good news of what the Lord
   has done!
All the sheep of Kedar and Nebaioth
Will be brought to you as sacrifices
And offered on the altar to please the Lord.
The Lord will make his Temple more glorious
   than ever.   (Isaiah 60:1-7 TEV)

The Lord says to Jerusalem,
"The wood of the pine, the juniper, and the
   cypress,
The finest wood from the forests of Lebanon,

Will be brought to rebuild you, Jerusalem,
To make my Temple beautiful,
To make my city glorious.
The sons of those who oppressed you will come
And bow low to show their respect.
All who once despised you will worship at your
   feet.
They will call you 'The City of the Lord,'
'Zion, the City of Israel's Holy God.'

"You will no longer be forsaken and hated,
A city deserted and desolate.
I will make you great and beautiful,
A place of joy forever and ever.
Nations and kings will care for you
As a mother nurses her child.
You will know that I, the Lord, have saved
   you,
That the mighty God of Israel sets you free.

"I will bring you gold instead of bronze,
Silver and bronze instead of iron and wood,
And iron instead of stone.
Your rulers will no longer oppress you;
I will make them rule with justice and peace.
The sounds of violence will be heard no more;
Destruction will not shatter your country again.
I will protect and defend you like a wall;
You will praise me because I have saved you."
                          (Isaiah 60:13-18 TEV)

17 In 445 B.C. Nehemiah
arrived in Jerusalem
to encourage the Jews
and supervise the rebuilding
of the walls of Jerusalem.

The seventy years that passed after the rebuilding of the Temple in Jerusalem were years of difficulties and disappointments for the exiles who had returned to their homeland. Darius had been succeeded on the throne of Persia first by Xerxes (486-465) and then by Artaxerxes I (465-423). The Persian authorities had blocked the attempts of the people in Jerusalem to reconstruct the city's walls, which badly needed repair. The great towers had been demolished; the remaining walls were breached by frequent gaps and in places leveled to the ground; the gates had been burned out. In those days, a city without walls was at the mercy of any enemy attack—and the Jews had plenty of

enemies, both inside and outside of the homeland that had been reoccupied at such great cost.

The man who restored the Jews' sagging spirits was Nehemiah, a Jew who had remained in Babylonia. He had risen to a prominent position in the Persian court—the cupbearer of the king. The cupbearer was a trusted official who was charged with responsibility for everything the king was given to drink and, particularly, for preventing him from being poisoned.

One day while Nehemiah was at the Persian winter capital at Susa serving the king and queen, the king noticed that his servant looked worried and sad; he privately asked him the reason for this. Nehemiah replied by sharing with the king the sad news he had received about the situation of the Jews in Jerusalem. The king permitted Nehemiah to travel to Jerusalem. He gave Nehemiah a letter guaranteeing safe travel to be shown to all local authorities along the way and a royal

decree allowing the walls of Jerusalem to be rebuilt. Nehemiah was himself named governor of Judea.

So in the year 445 B.C. Nehemiah arrived in Jerusalem, accompanied by a small armed escort. After inspecting the broken city walls during the night, he gathered the people together to persuade them to begin the rebuilding project; they enthusiastically agreed. Nehemiah skillfully recruited workers and then organized the workers into teams to work simultaneously on assigned sections of the walls; in this way the work made swift progress.

Soon neighboring states learned about the rebuilding of Jerusalem's walls. Sanballat, the governor of Samaria; Tobiah, leader of the Ammonites; and Geshem, chief of the Arabs in southern Judah, did not want Jerusalem to be refortified. They ridiculed the building effort and then threatened to stop it by force. To ward off these assaults, Nehemiah posted his own armed men around the area to defend the workers, who themselves were armed: "Even those who carried building materials worked with one hand and kept a weapon in the other, and everyone who was building kept a sword strapped to his waist" (Nehemiah 4:17-18 TEV).

In spite of these obstacles, the Jews managed to complete their work in fifty-two days of feverish activity. They then dedicated the walls and gates and celebrated with a feast.

The inhabitants of Jerusalem had other problems. The officials who had been appointed to govern the people had taken advantage of the community; they demanded that the people pay them more and more tribute. The rich managed to do so, but the poor were forced to borrow from others in order to meet the tribute payments, especially in the years when the harvests were scarce. The poor became burdened with heavy debts, and often had their fields taken for debt payment. Sometimes when they could no longer pay, they even had to give up their own children, who then became slaves.

As governor, Nehemiah intervened strongly. He cancelled debts and gave back to poor people whatever had been taken away. He set the example by refusing to accept the tribute due him as governor. Nehemiah's fair and honest leadership lasted for twelve years; after that, he returned to serve again King Artaxerxes in Persia.

18 Some years later Ezra
returned from exile
with hope of restoring
religious traditions
and faithfulness to God.

Nehemiah was very important in the restoration of the city of Jerusalem and also the Jewish nation. Another person—Ezra—was very important to the religious life of the Jewish people after the Exile. Ezra brought about a wide-ranging, deep religious reform that touched all aspects of Jewish life. He had lived in the Jewish community in Babylonia. He was both a priest and a member of the scribes, a new group of religious scholars that had begun in Babylonia. He had a reputation as "a scribe skilled in the law of Moses" (Ezra 7:6).

While yet in Babylon, Ezra studied and copied the religious texts that had been collected and organized during the long years of the Babylonian exile. He studied in particular the Law, that is, the Pentateuch, or first five books. In addition, he was able to interpret these ancient writings.

Ezra heard frequent reports about the condition of the Jews who had returned to Jerusalem. Through these reports, Ezra realized that many Jews there were ignorant of the law of God, and as a result they did not very strictly practice their religion.

Ezra had come into the good graces of the Persian King Artaxerxes (perhaps the second king with that name, who reigned between 404 and

358 B.C.), so he was able to obtain a royal decree that authorized him to travel to Jerusalem with as many returning exiles as he wanted to accompany him. The decree also allowed him to teach the written law there and appoint judges to enforce it. The Persian king and the wealthy Jews of Babylonia gave Ezra generous gifts of silver and gold to take to the Temple. The king told Ezra that he could use funds and goods from the treasury of the Persian province made up of Syria and Palestine in order to support official worship in the Temple. The priests who presided at the Temple worship and servants attached to the Temple would not be required to pay taxes.

Armed with this help and authority, Ezra set out to persuade as many capable people as possible, especially priests and Levites, to join him in emigrating back to Jerusalem. The Jewish community there was in special need of new blood, especially of those able to make a significant contribution to keeping alive Jewish traditions.

And so Ezra soon found himself at the head of a caravan of around eighteen hundred men accompanied by their entire families; there must have been at least five thousand people in all. This group possessed large quantities of silver, gold and other valuables. After a long journey they arrived safely in Jerusalem, where the people happily welcomed them. The gifts of the king and of the Babylonian Jewish community were presented, and the new arrivals immediately had their priests offer sacrifices in the Temple to the God of Israel.

Ezra was shocked to learn how far away from the Lord and his Law the people had fallen; he was especially upset to discover how many people—even leaders, who should have set a good example—had married foreigners, persons outside the Jewish community. He wanted to change people's minds and hearts and move them to repentance. To accomplish this, Ezra put on garments of mourning, fell upon his knees in the Temple and spread out his hands to the Lord, and, weeping, prayed for God's forgiveness for his people. A crowd of men, women, and children joined him in his prayer and wept bitterly for their sins. It was the beginning of an extensive and far-reaching religious reform, which affects the Jewish religion even today.

19 Ezra led the people in confessing their sins, renewing their covenant with God, and remembering they were the Chosen People.

In the early autumn, two months after his arrival, Ezra assembled all the people in the main square by the Water Gate in Jerusalem. He stood up where everybody could see and hear him. Then, after having pronounced a blessing on all the people—to which they replied, "Amen! Amen!"—he began to read the book of the Law so that the people would learn all that was contained in it and know they must obey it. Ezra read from dawn until mid-day. He read a few passages at a time, slowly and carefully, in Hebrew, the sacred language that few understood any longer. Some Levites stood around Ezra, and as he read, they translated into Aramaic, the commonly spoken language of the people; they also explained what was being read.

Probably the book Ezra read was Deuteronomy, with its strong pleas to be faithful and love the Lord "with all your heart, and with all your soul, and with all your might" (Deuteronomy 6:4) and with its vivid descriptions of the terrible punishments that awaited those who broke the Law. The people were deeply moved by this solemn proclamation of the Law, and many among them wept as they listened. So Ezra and the Levites reminded them: "This day is holy to the Lord your God, so you are not to mourn or cry. Now go home and have a feast. Share your food and wine with those who don't have enough. Today is

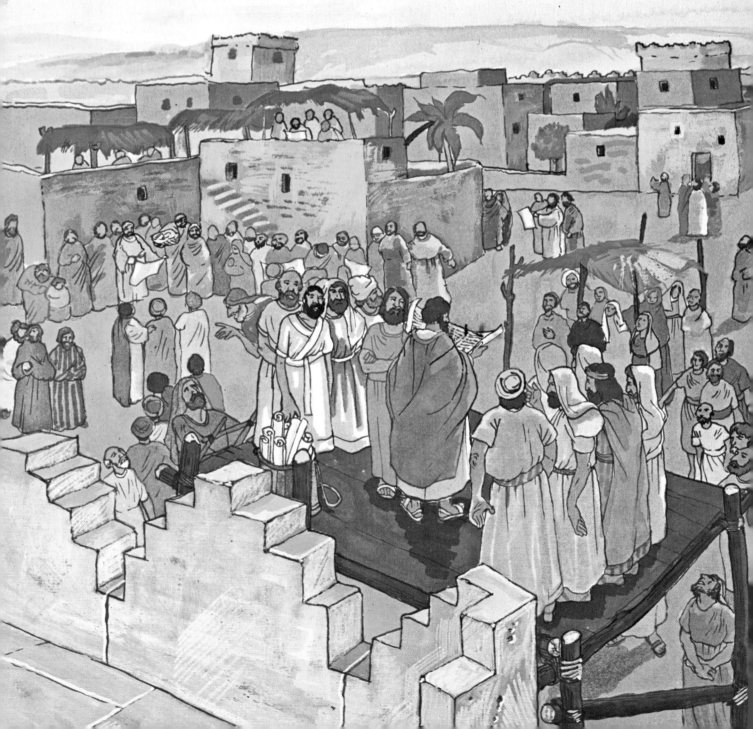

holy to our Lord, so don't be sad. The joy that the Lord gives you will make you strong" (Nehemiah 8:9-10 TEV).

The next day Ezra continued to instruct in the Law many priests, Levites, and heads of families. They learned that in two weeks it was time for the harvest festival, the Feast of Tabernacles, or Booths. Ezra ordered everybody to gather the leaves of olive, palm, and myrtle trees and out of them to construct huts for each family, to recall the time when the children of Israel lived in the wilderness after the Exodus from Egypt. This feast, which had not been celebrated for centuries, lasted for eight days, and each day Ezra had more portions of the Law read aloud.

After the festival, the people gathered to publicly confess their sins and to acknowledge that as a people they had been unfaithful to God, who had always been generous toward them. Then they renewed the covenant of Sinai between God and the people. In this renewal of the covenant, the Jews pledged to avoid mixed marriages, which destroyed the unity of the people; to keep holy the Sabbath day; to contribute annually to the upkeep of the Temple and its worship; to set aside tithes and firstfruits of harvest for religious purposes; and, in general, to be faithful to all the religious duties neglected up until then, either deliberately or out of ignorance.

From this time on, Judaism was characterized by deep respect for the Law. The Jews became noted for holding themselves apart as a people: They were the Chosen People of God, united by the Law and worship in the Temple, even though they still remained political subjects of the Persian emperor.

20 After the Exile
Jews became scattered
in many parts of the world
outside Palestine.
This scattering
was called the Diaspora.
Alexandria in Egypt
became one Jewish center.

Diaspora is a Greek word that means "dispersion." Greek-speaking Jews used this word to describe the Jewish communities that were scattered about, or dispersed, in the world outside Palestine after the Babylonian Exile. The first places settled by Jews were cities in the Persian Empire, then cities in the empire of Alexander the Great, and finally, in the Roman Empire. Even today the term Diaspora is used to describe the communities of Jews who live in cities throughout the world, particularly in Europe and America, as compared with those Jews who now live together in modern Israel.

The Diaspora began when Nebuchadnezzar deported many Jews to Babylonia in 587 B.C. After the Edict of Cyrus in 538 B.C., a sizable portion of Jews, though free to return to their homeland, did not do so. By then, many of them were well-off and preferred to remain in Babylon. It was at that time that the Jewish communities in exile became well organized. They were headed by leaders who stayed in touch with Jerusalem, which was still the people's religious center. These Jews in Babylon remained there for centuries, living in their own closed communities. They conducted business with their neighbors, but their way of living and worshiping was kept strictly apart from non-Jews.

Jewish communities became established in other parts of the Persian Empire besides the city of Babylon. From the stories of Esther and Tobit, it is clear that Jews lived in such cities as Susa and Ecbatana.

Egypt became another center for Jewish settlement. When many of the inhabitants of Judah were deported to Babylonia, a group of Jewish families also went down to Egypt, taking the prophet Jeremiah with them. We know that a Jewish military colony was established on the island of Elephantine on the upper Nile in the time of Darius II (423-404 B.C.).

The city of Alexandria, founded by Alexander the Great in 331 B.C., became an especially important center for thousands of Jews who were attracted by the business opportunities in this thriving new city. The Jews there, unlike those in Babylonia, were influenced by the Hellenistic, or Greek, culture in which they were living. But they still remained faithful to the religion of their ancestors and kept in close touch with Jerusalem.

From the port of Alexandria, ships traded with all the ports of the Mediterranean. As a result, some Jews ended up emigrating to the Greek cities of Asia Minor, to those on the North African coast such as Cyrene, and to those on the Syrian coast such as Antioch. Very quickly Jews had settled throughout the entire Roman Empire, including, of course, in Rome itself.

Since the Jews of the Diaspora were engaged in business, they were generally much better off materially than those who remained back in Judea. They spoke Greek and were citizens of the world. These dispersed Jewish communities were generally governed by a council of *archons* (rulers) for civil affairs and a head of the synagogue for religious affairs. The word *synagogue* was sometimes used to describe the whole community, and sometimes used to describe the meetinghouse of the Jewish religious community. The synagogue was the place where Jews gathered to pray together and to hear the reading of holy Scripture on the Sabbath and on feast days. Each year the various Jewish communities of the Diaspora sent generous donations to the Temple in Jerusalem.

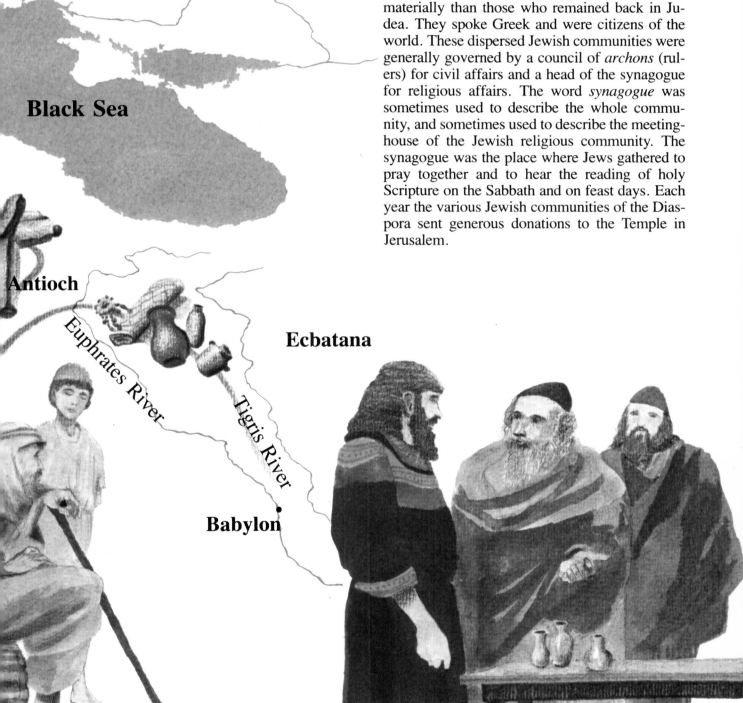

Black Sea

Antioch

Euphrates River

Tigris River

Ecbatana

Babylon

21 Some Hebrew Scripture is "wisdom literature." It is less concerned about history and gives more common-sense advice.

The Bible contains a number of books that are quite different from most of the others. These books are called "wisdom literature." They do not retell history, as do the books of Judges or Kings; they do not set forth the Law and the many religious rules based on it, as do the books of the Pentateuch from Exodus on; they do not contain warnings, threats, and promises, as do the books of the prophets. To summarize, they do not, in general, concern themselves with the past experiences of the Chosen People, as the other books of the Bible do. Rather, they try to teach people how to live an honest, orderly, and honorable life; they instruct people in "wise" living.

Wisdom literature began in the reign of Solomon, where court scribes began writing down many sayings that gave advice about living. Solomon himself took part in this effort. The wisdom literature of the Jews was heavily influenced by similar writings—particularly Egyptian models— popular throughout the ancient Near East. We possess Egyptian papyruses that contain collections of maxims and proverbs similar to those found in the Book of Proverbs in the Bible.

Wisdom literature does not set forth theory; rather it is based on everyday experience and practical, common sense knowledge. It gives advice on how to deal with the various problems that come up in the course of a human life. Usually written in the form of brief, often poetical verses, wisdom literature says that "the fear of God" is the beginning of wisdom.

The biblical proverbs were in most cases handed down orally over the years by the elders of the people. Later they were collected and written down by the scribes, those persons who could write and read. Often these scribes added other proverbs and developed existing ones, relying on their own experience of life.

In the fifth century B.C., following the Exile, the biblical Book of Proverbs was written down as we have it. Around this same time a marvelous book on the problem of pain and meaning in human life—the Book of Job—came into being. Later, around the third century B.C., came the pessimistic Book of Ecclesiastes, or "the Preacher." Then around the beginning of the second century B.C., a man named Jesus ben Sirach (or "son of Sirach") wrote the wisdom book known by the name Sirach, or Ecclesiasticus. This book put together ancient Near Eastern wisdom and revealed Hebrew religion, especially the Law of Moses; it reflected the writer's deep love of worship in the Temple.

Other wisdom writings are the Book of Wisdom (also called the Wisdom of Solomon, even though it was set down in writing in Alexandria) and the Song of Solomon (or Song of Songs), which celebrates married love as God had established it.

The very important Book of Psalms also belongs to the category of wisdom literature. However, the psalms are somewhat different—they are really prayers in poetic form.

In addition to the writings mentioned above, a number of books called historical books really belong to the category of wisdom literature. These are the Books of Ruth, Jonah, Tobit, Esther, and Judith.

Sirach and the Wisdom of Solomon are among a handful of books called deuterocanonical books. These books were not accepted into Scripture for some years by the ancient Christian church. Eventually Roman Catholic Christians accepted as part of the Bible all of the Old Testament deuterocanonical books, but most Protestant Christians did not include them. The other Old Testament books in this category are Baruch, Tobit, Judith, and 1 and 2 Maccabees—plus a few fragments of other books.

Even though most Protestant Christians do not consider the Old Testament deuterocanonical books to be inspired by God, most Protestants do study these books as important sources of information about Jewish life and traditions during the last few centuries before Jesus.

22
The Book of Proverbs
is a collection of sayings,
many of them
about wisdom and folly.

The Book of Proverbs was written by many different authors over a period of many years. The oldest parts of the book include two collections of proverbs said to be written by King Solomon and another collection known as "the sayings of wise men." The "wisdom" contained in these proverbs is firsthand wisdom acquired through experience; this kind of wisdom is universal and is not necessarily tied to any specific religion or people.

An appendix, tacked-on material, was added later to these three older collections; this appendix contains proverbs from some apparently non-Jewish sources. The book concludes with a poem in praise of the wise and active woman; this may have been added at an even later time.

The prologue, or beginning, of the Book of Proverbs, which makes up the first nine chapters, was certainly written after the Babylonian Exile. The writer reflects on how wisdom is related to God. In this prologue divine Wisdom is presented as though it were a person. This Wisdom, speaking with a divine voice, represents herself as coming into being before the creation of the world. The person Wisdom assisted God in the work of creation; now she wants to communicate herself to people, instructing the young as a mother or father would teach their children. The young are warned to avoid ways of living that lead to destruction and death, and instead are encouraged to follow wise advice that leads to a full life.

In the passage from the Book of Proverbs quoted below, Wisdom contrasts herself with Folly, also personified as a woman. Wisdom is the teacher of virtue and of an honest life based on "the fear of God." She presents her teaching as a banquet to whom she invites all who are inexperienced or "simple"; the inexperienced do not yet possess wisdom and are therefore in danger of making mistakes in their choice in life.

Folly, or the foolish woman, is set up in competition to Wisdom, and she pretends to be able to instruct people on how to live. However, she teaches that people should get ahead through dishonesty and cunning: "Stolen water is sweeter. Stolen bread tastes better" (Proverbs 9:17 TEV). In reality, though, the way of Folly is the way to death.

Here are the ways of Wisdom and Folly in the words of the Book of Proverbs:

Wisdom has built her house and made seven columns for it. She has had an animal killed for a feast, mixed spices in the wine, and set the table. She has sent her servant girls to call out from the highest place in town: "Come in, ignorant people!" And to the foolish man she says, "Come, eat my food and drink the wine that I have mixed. Leave the company of ignorant people, and live. Follow the way of knowledge." (Proverbs 9:1-6 TEV)

Stupidity is like a loud, ignorant, shameless woman. She sits at the door of her house or on a seat in the highest part of town, and calls out to people passing by, who are minding their own business: "Come in, ignorant people!" To the foolish man she says, "Stolen water is sweeter. Stolen bread tastes better." Her victims do not know that the people die who go to her house, that those who have already entered are now deep in the world of the dead.

(Proverbs 9:13-18 TEV)

23

People have always asked,
"Why do innocent people
suffer?"
The Book of Job deals
with this question
by retelling an old story.
Job, a man who was
innocent and faithful to God,
lost his health, his family,
and all his possessions.

Stories about innocent persons who suffer greatly have been told in many cultures throughout time. In Old Testament times various peoples told and passed down the story of a good and wise man unjustly afflicted with tremendous sufferings. This story is told in the Bible in the Book of Job. We do not know when or where the historical Job lived, or if there really was a historical Job. Modern scholars say that the core of the story of Job was first told in Phoenicia between the fifteenth and fourteenth centuries B.C. The story was handed down orally from parents to children and also handed on from tribe to tribe. The story thus came to the people of Israel, and around the eighth century B.C. an unknown Israelite wrote it down, changing it to fit Israel's idea of the one unique God. But this was not the final version of the story.

Around the beginning of the fifth century B.C., another Israelite author took up the story. He divided the old story in two and used it as a framework into which he inserted material about Job written in poetry. This verse portion, which makes up the greatest part of the present Book of Job, is a debate between Job and three friends, ranging over a number of topics.

A final part that was added to the Book of Job consists of a hymn to Wisdom and the speeches of a man called Elihu; this part was added to the poetic dialogue.

Even though the Book of Job was written over a period of time by several different writers, the parts of the book all work well together in dealing with a common theme of the just person who is afflicted by violence, misfortune, and suffering. The dramatic theme and subject matter of the Book of Job is the mystery of suffering by innocent persons. The Book of Job asks the question, Are these persons abandoned by God?

The first two chapters of the Book of Job, like the conclusion, are written in prose. These oldest parts of the book tell a simple story.

Job, a man who lived somewhere in the East, was both fortunate and prosperous. He had seven sons and three daughters and possessed many riches—so many that his children could count on enjoying happy and prosperous lives, except that Job's good fortune underwent a sudden, significant change. The change began when God looked over the whole world. God noted Job, a just and blameless man, free of any wrongdoing. God asked Satan, who was acting as a prosecuting attorney, if he, too, had seen Job. Satan was forced to answer that he had noticed Job. However, Satan added that Job was blameless only because he had everything. Job should be put to the test, and then it would be seen whether he would remain faithful or not.

The trials of Job began one day when his children were having a feast together, his herds of oxen were at pasture, and everything was in order. Suddenly the Sabeans, nomads from western Arabia, raided and stole his donkeys. An uninterrupted series of misfortunes followed: A fire destroyed both Job's sheep and shepherds; the Chaldeans destroyed his camels and drivers; a violent storm blew down the house where his children were feasting, and they were all buried underneath the rubble.

Finally, Job himself was afflicted with a disease which caused dreadful body sores. In spite of it all, Job continued to have faith in God, for his faith was not based on his having good fortune. "The Lord gave, and the Lord has taken away; blessed be the name of the Lord" (Job 1:21).

God permits evil and suffering, but it does not mean that God is hostile toward us. Rather, evil and suffering are a mystery, something that we cannot really understand. The chapters of Job that follow take a good look at that mystery in our lives.

24 Job asked God why persons
suffer and die.
God did not give simple answers
to all Job's questions.
But Job continued to believe
that God was good
and faithful to his promises.

The largest part of the Book of Job is the verses in the middle that present a debate between Job and three of his friends who have come to try and console him about his sufferings. This debate focuses on Job's own misfortunes, but it also examines the problem of suffering and death for human beings in general. Job wondered, why do human beings have to suffer and die? And why do the innocent and defenseless often suffer the most? Can it perhaps be that God is not just?

Job's friends thought his questions were shocking. They offered a convenient explanation to the problem of pain: The wicked are punished as they deserve to be, while the good are rewarded. If Job was afflicted by God, it must have been because he was guilty of some wrong; he needed to acknowledge his guilt and make up for it in some way in order to get back his good fortune.

Job, however, knew that he was innocent. The suffering that he was undergoing taught him that the innocent do suffer. This brought him face to face with a dramatic choice. He could deny what he knew to be true—that he was innocent—and say that he was indeed guilty, along with all others who suffer. Or he could admit that the innocent do suffer unjustly, due to the fact that God is unjust. Job rebelled against both of these conclusions. On the one hand, he knew that he was indeed innocent; on the other hand, he knew with equal certainty that God was good and faithful to his promises.

Job rejected the temptation to blame God, which from time to time became very strong for him. At the same time, he passionately begged God to intervene and demonstrate his power. Job realized that compared to God, human beings are nothing. Our lives are short, like those of a flower. So why

worry about a creature who at any moment may be cut down by death, with no possibility of escaping? We do not know what Job believed about life after death, but he seemed to think that after death God would give him justice.

We are all born weak and helpless.
All lead the same short, troubled life.
We grow and wither as quickly as flowers;
we disappear like shadows.
Will you even look at me, God,
or put me on trial and judge me?
Nothing clean can ever come
from anything as unclean as man.
The length of his life is decided beforehand—
the number of months he will live.
You have settled it, and it can't be changed.
Look away from him and leave him alone;
let him enjoy his hard life—if he can.

There is hope for a tree that has been cut down;
it can come back to life and sprout.
Even though its roots grow old,
and its stump dies in the ground,
with water it will sprout like a young plant.
But a man dies, and that is the end of him;
he dies, and where is he then?

Like rivers that stop running,
and lakes that go dry,
people die, never to rise.
They will never wake up while the sky endures;
they will never stir from their sleep.
I wish you would hide me in the world of the dead;
let me be hidden until your anger is over,
and then set a time to remember me.
If a man dies, can he come back to life?
But I will wait for better times,
wait till this time of trouble is ended.
Then you will call, and I will answer.
(Job 14:1-15 TEV)

25 In the end, Job was satisfied
to admit that he was
just a human being
and not God.
He placed himself
completely in God's hands.

Upset by his friends' lack of understanding, Job more than once called upon God for answers. Finally God spoke, but did not answer Job's questions exactly as Job had asked them. Instead, Job was shown just who God was—stronger and wiser than human beings, who could not in any way compare with God.

Then is given God's own set of questions of Job: How many things are there that human beings simply did not know? How many things are there that are simply beyond our comprehension? Where was Job when God created the world, set boundaries to the seas, and decided the order of the seasons? Who created all earth's animals and provided for them?

God's reply was not what Job had wanted or expected. Nevertheless, he did understand the meaning of the reply. Humans are not equal to God nor can we ask for an accounting for God's actions. When we realize who God is, it is best to recognize God's superior wisdom and power and simply stand in silence before it.

Except for assertions about divine knowledge and power, God did not really answer Job's questions. Job, however, humbled himself before God and did not argue anymore. Job recognized that God's very wisdom and power gave him reason to trust and hope. If God had the power to overcome evil, injustice, and suffering and yet permitted all these things anyway, it must mean that these things had a meaning that human beings simply could not see. And so Job, understanding what it was to be a human being and not God, placed himself in the hands of God:

> You ask how I dare question your wisdom
> when I am so very ignorant.
> I talked about things I did not understand,
> about marvels too great for me to know.
> Then I knew only what others had told me,
> but now I have seen you with my own eyes.
> (Job 42:3, 5 TEV)

Job's prayer was not useless, and his debate with his friends was not without reward. As a result of what he learned, Job learned what is true faith: putting oneself completely in God's hands.

And God did not abandon his faithful one. God intervened and gave Job back a better life. He gave Job greater prosperity than before he was tested. The suffering of the innocent always has value in God's eyes, but God does not necessarily always reward the just in this world.

26

The author
of the Book of Jonah
was trying to tell the Jews
that God cared about
people of all nations.
In the story of Jonah,
God commanded Jonah
to preach to Nineveh.
Jonah tried to flee from God
by boat,
but he was thrown overboard
and was swallowed
by a great fish.

The Book of Jonah is placed among the books of the prophets in the Bible. In fact, however, this book does not contain any prophecy, that is, a message from God for a certain historical situation. Instead, it tells a story that is intended to teach a moral lesson. The story of Jonah was written down by an Israelite of the fifth century B.C. In order to give greater importance to the story, this fifth-century author gave the book the name of Jonah, a prophet of the eighth century B.C.

The book was made up of two separate incidents, both of which were intended to teach the same lesson. This lesson was that God's mercy was not limited to the Chosen People—God was merciful towards everybody. The author of the Book of Jonah was trying to warn the Jews about being too exclusive. The small Jewish community, surrounded as it was by stronger peoples on all sides, was in danger of turning in too much upon itself. The Book of Jonah was written to demonstrate that although Israel was the Chosen People, God's mercy really extended to all people, and even to plants and animals.

The author of the Book of Jonah had a fine sense of humor. He made gentle fun of Jonah, who took himself too seriously. The author also revealed great sympathy for those pagans who were honest and who feared God. The story of Jonah begins with a command from God to the prophet Jonah: Go preach to Nineveh, the great city of the Assyrians, a city known for its evil ways. Terrified by the difficulty of this mission, Jonah took off in the opposite direction and headed towards the port of Jaffa. There he boarded a boat headed towards Tarshish, a city located in southern Spain (which for the Hebrews represented the end of the earth). Jonah imagined that by fleeing so far away he would be able to escape from God's sight and power.

Jonah was mistaken. God raised up a fierce wind, which caused a furious storm. The sailors on Jonah's ship were terrified; each one turned to his own god, asking for help. The sailors also began throwing cargo overboard. All this while, Jonah lay in a deep sleep in one corner of the ship. There he was spotted by the captain, who cried out to him, "What do you mean, you sleeper? Arise, call upon your god! Perhaps the god will give a thought to us that we do not perish" (Jonah 1:6).

The captain and the sailors realized that divine power stood behind this storm. They decided to draw lots in order to identify the person who had angered heaven. Needless to say, the lot fell to Jonah. Confronted with his guilt, Jonah described to all the divine command and his attempt to escape it. Jonah then said to the sailors, "Take me up and throw me into the sea; then the sea will quiet down for you" (Jonah 1:12).

After praying to God, the sailors did as Jonah told them, and they threw him overboard. The sea became calm. Jonah, however, was not abandoned by God. He was swallowed by a great fish and passed three days and nights in the belly of the fish. Finally the fish spit him out on the beach.

This incident taught the lesson that when things seem to get so bad that they are past all hope, God intervenes with a remedy. As a result of his experience in the belly of the fish, Jonah in a beautiful prayer thanked God for deliverance.

From deep inside the fish Jonah prayed
to the Lord his God:

"In my distress, O Lord, I called to you,
    and you answered me.
From deep in the world of the dead
    I cried for help, and you heard me.
You threw me down into the depths,
    to the very bottom of the sea,
    where the waters were all around me,
    and all your mighty waves rolled over me.
I thought I had been banished from your presence
    and would never see your holy Temple again.
The water came over me and choked me;
    the sea covered me completely,
    and seaweed wrapped around my head.
I went down to the very roots of the mountains,
    into the land whose gates lock shut forever.
But you, O Lord my God,
    brought me back from the depths alive.
When I felt my life slipping away,
    then, O Lord, I prayed to you,
    and in your holy Temple you heard me.
Those who worship worthless idols
    have abandoned their loyalty to you.
But I will sing praises to you;
    I will offer you a sacrifice
    and do what I have promised.
Salvation comes from the Lord!"
                    (Jonah 2:1-9 TEV)

27

After he escaped from the fish,
Jonah went to preach
to the people of Nineveh.
When the people of Nineveh
repented, Jonah scolded God
for being merciful.
But Jonah, through his pity
for a dying plant,
came to understand
the mercy of God.

After Jonah's disobedience, God repeated the order to Jonah to go preach to Nineveh. Jonah had no choice except to go as God had commanded, so this time he obeyed and went to the capital of the Assyrians.

The author of the Book of Jonah probably did not really know much about what Nineveh was like. Nineveh had been destroyed by the Babylonians in 612 B.C., around two centuries before this book was written. But very likely the author had heard tales about the city's wickedness and its great size and splendor. He described it as a very large city that required three days to cross.

Jonah did as he had been told and spent the first three days walking through the city preaching that God's anger was coming upon the city. Within forty days Nineveh would be destroyed. Those who heard his words were frightened. Someone even reported them to the king, who was badly shaken by them. The king came down from his throne and dressed himself in garments meant for doing penance; then he issued a decree ordering all the inhabitants of the city, humans and animals as well, to fast and do penance. If the people repented, perhaps God would spare the city.

The city was, in fact, spared. God saw the good will of the inhabitants of Nineveh and laid aside his plans to punish the city. Jonah was furious at this outcome. He had feared that things would turn out just that way. That is why he had originally tried to flee. Jonah said to God: "I knew that you are a loving and merciful god, always patient, always kind, and always ready to change your mind and not punish" (Jonah 4:2 TEV).

Jonah was scolding God for being merciful! By having Jonah make this silly complaint to God, the author is really pointing out how ridiculous it is for some of the members of the Jewish community to regularly call upon God to punish all

the pagans. Should God not have been merciful? Was not the real purpose of punishment to bring about repentance in the hearts of sinners? God is loving toward all his creatures. God reminded Jonah of this.

Jonah went outside the city. He constructed a kind of hut for himself to protect himself from the scorching hot sun. In order to protect Jonah even better, the Lord caused a plant to grow up rapidly; its shade pleased Jonah a great deal.

The following day, however, the plant dried out and died. Once again, Jonah complained to God.

The Lord said to him, "This plant grew up in one night and disappeared the next; you didn't do anything for it and you didn't make it grow— yet you feel sorry for it! How much more, then, should I have pity on Nineveh, that great city. After all, it has more than 120,000 innocent children in it, as well as many animals!"

(Jonah 4:10-11 TEV)

The Book of Jonah ends with this question God asks Jonah. The Jewish author of this book has revealed some important truths about God's nature and his mercy, truths that Jesus would reveal again later.

28

The Book of Ruth tells how
Ruth, a Gentile woman,
loved Naomi,
her Jewish mother-in-law.
After Ruth's husband died,
she left her own people and
went to Palestine with Naomi.

In the story of Ruth, a Moabite woman shows great loyalty and love for Naomi, her mother-in-law, and through this devotion becomes a member of the Chosen People and David's great-grand-mother. Written by an anonymous author, the Book of Ruth contains some material that is probably very ancient. Most scholars believe the Book of Ruth was written down after the Babylonian Exile, although the story itself takes place around 1100 B.C., several generations before David.

The content of this book resembles that of both Job and Jonah. All three stories deal with God's action in the lives of human beings who have their faithfulness and loyalty tested. Since the Book of Ruth describes the virtues of a pagan woman, scholars think it may have been written down when it was in order to counteract a Jewish movement toward staying clear of all other peoples.

The story told in the Book of Ruth took place during the time of the judges. In those days there was a terrible famine. As a result, an Israelite named Elimelech, a native of Bethlehem, decided to emigrate to Moab, a country to the southeast of Judah that was a centuries-long enemy of the Israelites. In spite of those old hostilities, Elimelech was able to establish himself in the Moabite countryside, along with his wife Naomi and their two sons, Mahlon and Chilion. Elimelech died; his two sons married local Moabite women, Orphah and Ruth. Nearly ten years passed, and then both Mahlon and Chilion died, too.

Crushed, Naomi decided to return to her own country; she had heard that the famine in Israel was long over. So she said to her widowed daughters-in-law: "Go, return each of you to her mother's house. May the Lord deal kindly with you, as you have dealt with the dead and with me" (Ruth 1:8).

The responses of her daughters-in-law were surprising to Naomi. They preferred to leave their families, their countries, and the possibility of new marriages in order to return to Israel with their

mother-in-law, whom they evidently loved greatly. Out of concern for them, however, Naomi insisted that they should return to their own families. (In these days women were thought of mainly as wives and mothers; almost all men and women were married, and the life of a woman depended very much on her husband.) She had no way to ensure a future for her daughters-in-law.

Finally, Orpah agreed to go back to her family. Ruth, however, would not change her mind. In response to Naomi's pleading, Ruth replied, "Entreat me not to leave you or to return from following you; for where you go I will go, and where you lodge I will lodge; your people shall be my people, and your God my God" (Ruth 1:16).

Naomi was persuaded by Ruth's words, and the two women set out for Judea. They came to Bethlehem, the home of Naomi, where many still remembered the widow of Elimelech and held

feasts to welcome her. Naomi told them about her misfortunes.

The two women had to find some work in order to live. It was summer, the season when barley was harvested in Israel. Taking advantage of a custom that allowed the poor to follow the reapers in the barley fields and glean, or gather, grain left on the ground, Ruth set to work as a gleaner.

It so happened—perhaps because it was God's plan—that Ruth, the Moabite woman, went to work in the fields of a man named Boaz, a rich landowner who was related to Naomi's husband, Elimelech. Boaz had heard about the misfortunes of his relative Naomi and about Ruth's devotion to her mother-in-law. Impressed by Ruth's loyalty, Boaz ordered his men to treat her with respect—and even to drop grain intentionally where she was gleaning. He personally spoke to Ruth, inviting her to return to his fields to glean.

29

Ruth picked grain in the fields
of Boaz, a relative of Naomi.
Boaz came to love Ruth
and followed the customs
of his time to get the right
to marry her.
David, the great-grandson
of Ruth and Boaz,
would become
the most famous king of Israel.

Responding to the invitation of Boaz, Ruth went out several days to glean in his fields, always leaving them with generous amounts of grain. Naomi noticed Boaz's interest in her daughter-in-law, and at the end of the harvest she went to Ruth and explained the common custom of the "levirate" marriage, which was meant to insure the security of childless widows and provide the family with descendants. Under it, the widow could expect to be married by her dead husband's brother, or the next closest relative if no brother existed. The first son born of this new marriage counted as a child of the dead husband. Since Naomi was too old for childbearing, perhaps Boaz would marry Ruth and continue the family line of Elimelech.

Naomi instructed Ruth about what to do. That night Boaz would be sleeping on his threshing floor (the place where the grain was separated from the straw), guarding the barley being harvested. Ruth was to wait until Boaz had retired for the night, then she was to go to him and lay herself down at his feet.

Ruth followed her mother-in-law's directions. When she was sure that Boaz was asleep, she approached, raised a corner of his cover, and lay down at his feet. In the night Boaz awoke and realized that there was a woman at his feet. At first he was amazed, but then he realized that the young Moabite woman was turning to him for the protection of a levirate marriage. He was willing to marry her, but there was one obstacle in the way. Among Elimelech's kinsmen was another who was a closer relative than Boaz was; this person would have to give up his right before Boaz himself could marry Ruth.

Early in the morning, therefore, Boaz sent Ruth away with a generous gift of barley. He himself went down to the city gates where the elders of the tribe regularly met. Eventually, the relative with the first right to marry Ruth arrived. Boaz told him that Naomi wanted to sell a field that had belonged to Elimelech. The closest relative had the right to buy it, but along with this right came the duty to marry Ruth in order to continue the family. Faced suddenly with the prospect of an unforeseen marriage which he had not planned on, the relative removed his sandal and gave it to Boaz; this was the sign that he was giving over to Boaz his rights in the matter. This was exactly what Boaz had wanted. He called the elders to witness his commitment to buy the field from Naomi and to marry Ruth.

The marriage of Boaz and Ruth was celebrated, and the Lord soon made their union fruitful and happy by the birth of a son, who was given the name of Obed. The entire family was full of joy. Naomi was especially happy, for her family was reborn. This family was destined to play an important role in the history of salvation, for Obed became the father of Jesse, who was the father of David the king. In this way, the Moabite woman Ruth became an ancestor of the kings of Israel, the dynasty from which the Messiah was to be born.

Another lesson was to be learned from this story: If a virtuous woman such as Ruth could actually attain such a high position in Israel even though she was a foreigner, Israel ought to reconsider its policy of isolating itself from and hating the surrounding peoples.

30 The prophet Joel announced
"the day of the Lord,"
when God would judge the world.
He also spoke of
future prosperity and
God's spirit being poured out
on all God's people.

The prophet Joel was the son of a man named
Pethuel. Other than that, the Bible tells nothing,
so no one knows when he lived and preached.
From the study of his writing style, some modern
biblical scholars have concluded that he lived and
worked around 350 B.C.

The Book of Joel can be divided into two parts
that are quite distinct from one another. In the first
part, the prophet described in very vivid and dramatic words the invasion of a plague of locusts,
which he interpreted as a punishment from God.
The locusts came in great swarms, blocked out
the sun, and ate everything in the land. They were
like a conquering army; it was impossible to escape from them. The only hope for the people was
to repent and do penance. If they repented, the
prophet said, God would stop his punishment. Joel
urged all the people and priests to repent in their
hearts.

In the second part of the book, the words of the
prophet became even more dramatic. He announced "the day of the Lord"—the day when
the Lord would judge the world and all the people
in it. Both the sun and the moon would become
pale in comparison with God's majesty, and the
stars would lose their splendor. The enemies of
Judah would be struck down without hope of
escape.

Judah, however, would once again become a
Promised Land. Her mountains would produce
new wines, and milk would flow abundantly among
her hills, and her streams would never dry up.
Joel also described the pouring out of the spirit of
prophecy upon the entire people of God so that all
would better see God's truth. Many years later, in
the biblical book called the Acts of the Apostles,
Peter would say that this prophecy of Joel had
been fulfilled when the Holy Spirit descended upon
the people on Pentecost.

Here are some of the prophet Joel's words:

Invitation to Repentance
"But even now," says the Lord,
  "repent sincerely and return to me
  with fasting and weeping and mourning.
Let your broken heart show your sorrow;
  tearing your clothes is not enough."
Come back to the Lord your God.
  He is kind and full of mercy;
  he is patient and keeps his promise;
  he is always ready to forgive and not punish.
Perhaps the Lord your God will change his mind
  and bless you with abundant crops.
Then you can offer him grain and wine.
  (Joel 2:12-14 TEV)

The Pouring Out of the Spirit
"Afterward I will pour out my spirit on everyone:
  your sons and daughters will proclaim my
    message;
  your old men will have dreams,
  and your young men will see visions.
At that time I will pour out my spirit
  even on servants, both men and women.

"I will give warnings of that day
  in the sky and on the earth;
  there will be bloodshed, fire, and clouds of
    smoke.
The sun will be darkened,
  and the moon will turn red as blood
  before the great and terrible day of the Lord
    comes.
But all who ask the Lord for help will be saved.
As the Lord has said,
  'Some in Jerusalem will escape;
  those whom I choose will survive.' "
  (Joel 2:28-32 TEV)

31 The Song of Songs,
or Song of Solomon,
is a collection
of beautiful love songs
about a man and a woman.
The love expressed here
reminds some readers
of the love between God
and God's Chosen People.

The Song of Songs, also known as the Song of Solomon or the Canticle of Canticles, is a collection of beautiful love songs similar to those that sometimes were used at Jewish weddings. The songs celebrated the faithfulness of the lovers to each other.

The Song of Songs has been interpreted in various ways. In one common interpretation, it is seen as a narrative of King Solomon, a beautiful maiden, and her shepherd lover. Chosen by Solomon to be one of his wives, the maiden is forced to live in his court, where the ladies of the court encourage her to accept his love. The lover comes to visit and encourages his beloved from outside the gates.

Even when praised by Solomon, the maiden thinks only of her absent lover. She dreams of seeing him again and tells her dream to the court ladies. Finally, Solomon understands what she really wants, and he releases her to go back to rejoin her lover. She then returns to him in the country, where they live happily ever after.

In this poetic drama, the maiden is the Jewish people in exile; Solomon represents the temptation of the people to idolatry, especially when they come in contact with the powerful Babylonian civilization. The lover is God, who visits his people through the prophets. The people (the maiden) remain faithful to their divine lover (God).

The Visit of the Lover
The voice of my beloved!
  Behold, he comes,
leaping upon the mountains,
  bounding over the hills.
My beloved is like a gazelle,
  or a young stag.
Behold, there he stands
  behind our wall,
gazing in at the windows,
  looking through the lattice.
My beloved speaks and says to me:
"Arise, my love, my fair one,
  and come away;
for lo, the winter is past,
  the rain is over and gone.
The flowers appear on the earth,
  the time of singing has come,
and the voice of the turtledove
  is heard in our land.
The fig tree puts forth its figs,
  and the vines are in blossom;
  they give forth fragrance.
Arise, my love, my fair one,
  and come away.
O my dove, in the clefts of the rock,
  in the covert of the cliff,
let me see your face,
  let me hear your voice,
for your voice is sweet,
  and your face is comely."
(Song of Solomon 2:8-14)

A Dream

Upon my bed by night
   I sought him whom my soul loves;
I sought him, but found him not;
   I called him, but he gave no answer.
"I will rise now and go about the city,
   in the streets and in the squares;
I will seek him whom my soul loves."
   I sought him, but found him not.
The watchmen found me,
   as they went about in the city.
"Have you seen him whom my soul loves?"
Scarcely had I passed them,
   when I found him whom my soul loves.
I held him, and would not let him go
   until I had brought him into my
      mother's house,
   and into the chamber of her that
      conceived me.
           (Song of Solomon 3:1-4)

The Triumph of Love

Set me as a seal upon your heart,
   as a seal upon your arm;
for love is strong as death,
   jealousy is cruel as the grave.
Its flashes are flashes of fire,
   a most vehement flame.
Many waters cannot quench love,
   neither can floods drown it.
If a man offered for love
   all the wealth of his house,
   it would be utterly scorned.
           (Song of Solomon 8:6-7)

32

The Book of Tobit tells the story
of Tobit, a faithful Jew,
and his son Tobias.
When Tobit became blind
and thought he would die soon,
Tobias went on a long trip
to collect a debt for his father.
On the trip he caught
a miraculous fish
and kept part of it.

The Book of Tobit is included among the historical books of the Bible, although it is a work meant more to inspire than to transmit exact history. In fact, the author of the book takes many liberties with both history and geography. Probably this writer lived in the third century B.C.

The book is not recognized as one of the authentic books of the Bible by either the Jews or Protestant Christians. However, the Book of Tobit is studied by all because it contains valuable teaching and explains a number of beliefs and traditions popular among Jews of the time. The book shows how close God remained to his people who continued to observe his law even though they were in exile from their homeland. The book teaches about almsgiving and respect for the dead. It also treats marriage and the family with great respect. In fact, it anticipates the teaching of Jesus on some of these subjects.

The story told in the Book of Tobit begins in the city of Nineveh between 725 and 650 B.C. — the time of great Assyrian power. The heroes of the story are Tobit, an Israelite carried off to Nineveh during the deportation from Israel ordered by Tiglath-Pileser III in 733 B.C.; his wife Anna; and his son Tobias.

Tobit had remained faithful to the Law of God even while in exile. For this reason God helped him, and he gained the trust of the Assyrian king Shalmaneser, who hired him as a buyer of supplies in Media, a land to the east of Assyria. On a trip to Rages in Media, Tobit loaned ten talents of silver to Gabael, a kinsman who lived there. When after some years Sennacherib became king, the roads to Media were no longer under Assyrian control, and Tobit was not able to travel there to collect what was owed him.

Tobit was a devout Jew; he performed many good acts for those around him—gave food and clothes to the poor, gave a proper burial to any Jew found dead and abandoned. Tobit had once angered the Assyrian king by these burials and had been expelled from Nineveh. But after he had been allowed to return, on one occasion he once again took steps to bury a murdered Israelite when informed of his death by his son Tobias. Tobit immediately went to the murder scene, took the body of the murdered Israelite, and buried the man after dark. His neighbors jeered at him for this.

Back home, Tobit went to sleep next to the walls of the courtyard. (It was not unusual to sleep outside during some seasons of the year.) During the night some bird droppings fell right into his eyes.

This absurd misfortune turned into tragedy: Tobit's eyes became infected and he went blind. What made his blindness even worse was the mockery of his neighbors, and even that of his own wife, Anna, who said: "Where are your charities and your righteous deeds?" (Tobit 2:14)

Tobit endured all this with patience. Believing his death was near, he called his son Tobias to him to tell him to honor his mother, take pity on the poor and needy, and remain faithful to the God of Abraham, Isaac, and Jacob. Then Tobit informed Tobias about the old loan of ten talents to Gabael of Rages in Media. Now it was time for Tobias to go to Rages to reclaim this money.

At that time a journey from Nineveh to Babylonia was neither easy nor safe. Tobias sought someone to be his guide. At this point God sent his angel Raphael to Tobias in the form of a knowledgeable and reliable young Israelite. Tobias chose him as a traveling companion. When Tobias left, Tobit blessed him, Anna wept, and the family dog chased after him to travel with him.

The journey, under God's protection, went very well. When they camped along the Tigris, Tobias went down to the river to wash his feet. A huge fish leapt out of the water. Tobias was frightened and wanted to run away, but the angel exhorted him not to be afraid. On the contrary, Tobias was instructed by Raphael to catch the fish, because the inner organs of the fish had properties that could cure his father Tobit of his blindness.

Tobias therefore caught the fish, and the two extracted its organs. They went on the road again with renewed faith.

33

While on the journey,
Tobias met Sarah.
Sure that God would bless them,
Tobias married Sarah, whose
earlier fiances had all died.
Safely back home,
Tobias used part of the fish
to cure his father's blindness.

On their way to Rages in the northeast of Media, Tobias and the angel passed through Ecbatana, the capital of ancient Media. In this community lived a man called Raguel, an Israelite and a kinsman of Tobias. Raphael suggested that they stay with Raguel; this stop was necessary to fulfill God's plan that Tobias should meet and marry Sarah, the daughter of Raguel. The angel mentioned to Tobias the possibility of marrying Sarah.

Tobias, however, had already heard about the strange fate that had pursued this daughter of Raguel. Sarah had already been engaged seven times, but her fiances had all mysteriously died on their wedding nights. A demon was jealous of Sarah and saw to it that no man ever got close to her.

Raphael reassured Tobias, saying that the power of God would defeat the demon. And so Tobias and Raphael went to see Raguel, who received them with great honor. After greetings, Raphael asked Raguel for Sarah's hand in marriage to Tobias. Raguel easily consented, and, according to the custom of the time, called Sarah and gave her to Tobias with these words: "Here she is; take her according to the Law of Moses, and take her with you to your father. ...The merciful God will guide you both for the best" (Tobit 7:13, 12).

Raguel was fearful about the wedding night, but Tobias had confidence in the word of his friend Raphael. After the wedding he and Sarah went to the bedroom. There Tobias followed exactly the

instructions Raphael had given him to burn the heart and the liver of the fish he had caught in the Tigris. Then Tobias and Sarah prayed confidently to God. After that the newlyweds were able to sleep without disturbances.

Raguel was so worried that he had even ordered a grave dug to receive Tobias. At the first light of dawn, he sent a servant to check on the newlyweds; the servant returned to say that the young couple were sleeping an untroubled sleep. Raguel was so pleased at this news that he ordered feasting to last for fourteen days.

It was time for Tobias to get back to Nineveh. He knew that his parents were anxiously awaiting his return. He felt obliged, however, to accept the invitation of his father-in-law to the feast. So he asked Raphael to go on to Rages. Raphael immediately agreed, went on to Rages, and returned with the money that had been lent. When the feasting ended, a small caravan left Ecbatana for Nineveh. In the caravan were Tobias, Raphael, and Sarah, along with servants and camels to transport her dowry (the goods and money a bride gave her husband when they were married).

When they reached the gates of Nineveh, Raphael ordered the caravan to stop. He and Tobias proceeded alone towards Tobit's house. The meeting between Tobias and his parents was full of emotions. Anna had been impatiently watching down the street for her son to arrive. When she saw Tobias in the distance, she hurried to tell Tobit. then she ran back and threw herself into Tobias's arms. When the blind Tobit reached them, the angel told Tobias to smear some of the bile from the fish's organs on his father's eyes. Miraculously, Tobit recovered his sight at once.

Now that he had his sight back, Tobit was able to follow his son to the gates of the city, where he became acquainted with his daughter-in-law. Still more wedding celebrations were held. Then Tobit and Tobias wanted to reward Raphael for all his help. Then Raphael finally revealed his true identity to them. As he dissolved into the air, Raphael begged Tobit and Tobias to remain always faithful and to thank God for his generosity.

"Praise God and give thanks to him; exalt him and give thanks to him in the presence of all the living for what he has done for you. It is good to praise God and to exalt his name, worthily declaring the works of God. Do not be slow to give him thanks." (Tobit 12:6)

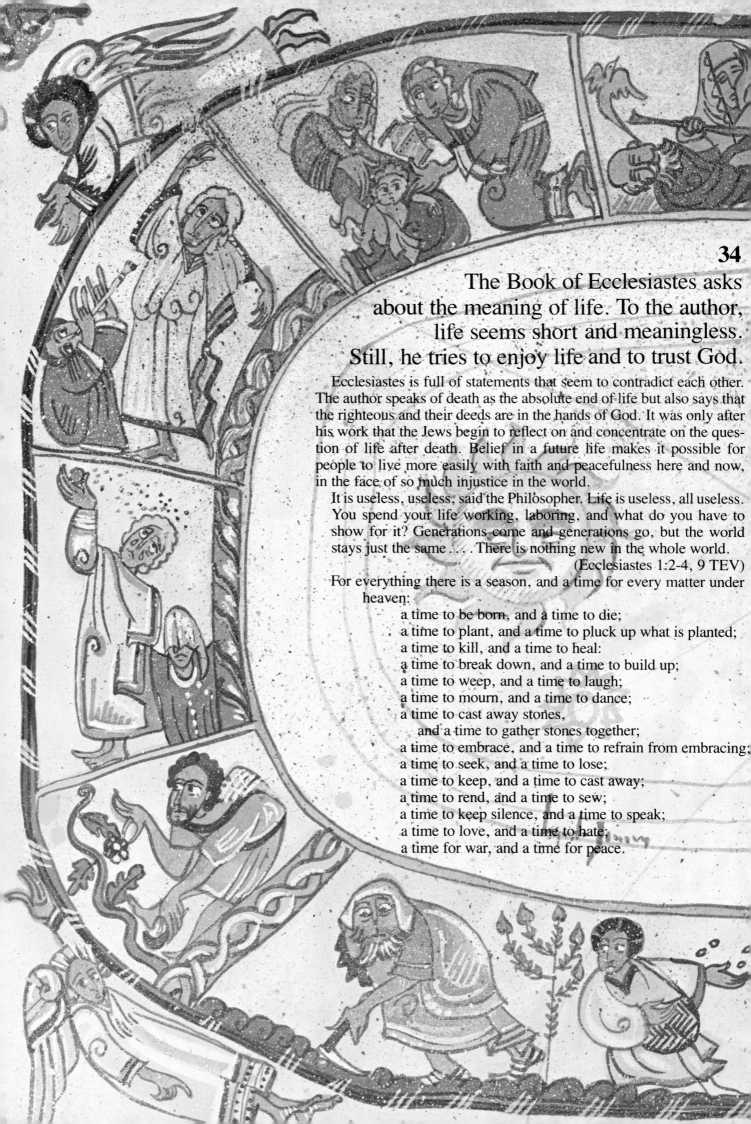

34

The Book of Ecclesiastes asks about the meaning of life. To the author, life seems short and meaningless. Still, he tries to enjoy life and to trust God.

Ecclesiastes is full of statements that seem to contradict each other. The author speaks of death as the absolute end of life but also says that the righteous and their deeds are in the hands of God. It was only after his work that the Jews begin to reflect on and concentrate on the question of life after death. Belief in a future life makes it possible for people to live more easily with faith and peacefulness here and now, in the face of so much injustice in the world.

It is useless, useless, said the Philosopher. Life is useless, all useless. You spend your life working, laboring, and what do you have to show for it? Generations come and generations go, but the world stays just the same .... There is nothing new in the whole world.

(Ecclesiastes 1:2-4, 9 TEV)

For everything there is a season, and a time for every matter under heaven:

a time to be born, and a time to die;
a time to plant, and a time to pluck up what is planted;
a time to kill, and a time to heal;
a time to break down, and a time to build up;
a time to weep, and a time to laugh;
a time to mourn, and a time to dance;
a time to cast away stones,
  and a time to gather stones together;
a time to embrace, and a time to refrain from embracing;
a time to seek, and a time to lose;
a time to keep, and a time to cast away;
a time to rend, and a time to sew;
a time to keep silence, and a time to speak;
a time to love, and a time to hate;
a time for war, and a time for peace.

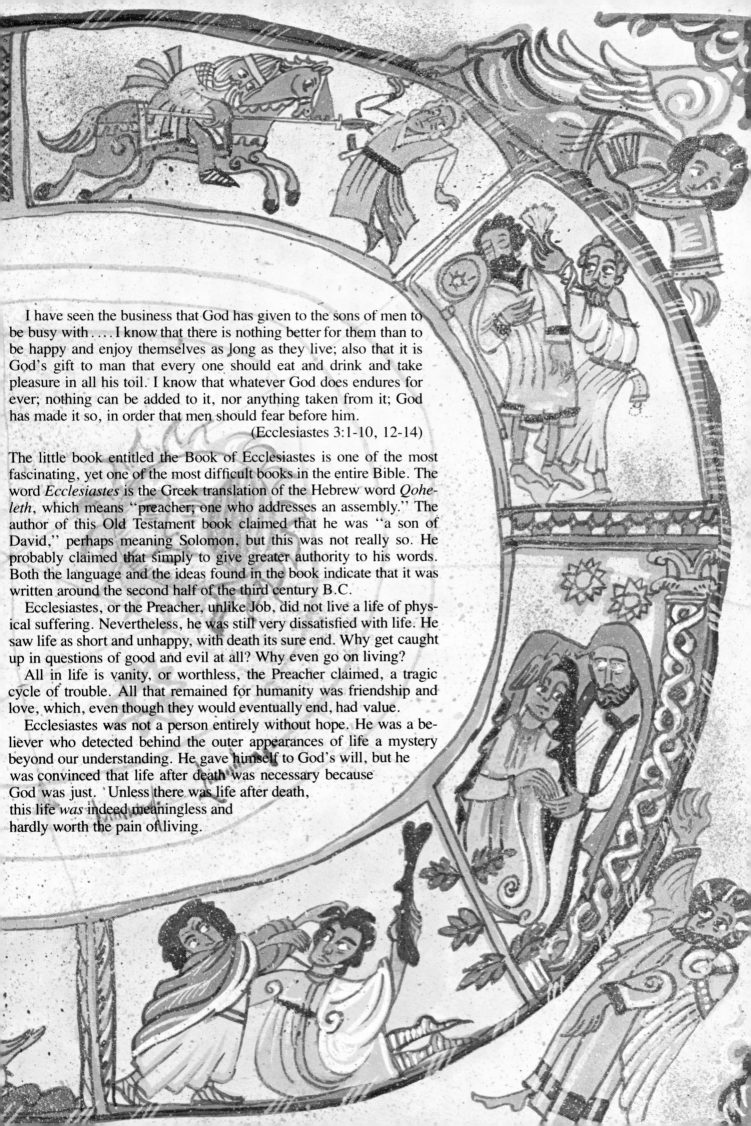

I have seen the business that God has given to the sons of men to be busy with . . . . I know that there is nothing better for them than to be happy and enjoy themselves as long as they live; also that it is God's gift to man that every one should eat and drink and take pleasure in all his toil. I know that whatever God does endures for ever; nothing can be added to it, nor anything taken from it; God has made it so, in order that men should fear before him.

(Ecclesiastes 3:1-10, 12-14)

The little book entitled the Book of Ecclesiastes is one of the most fascinating, yet one of the most difficult books in the entire Bible. The word *Ecclesiastes* is the Greek translation of the Hebrew word *Qoheleth*, which means "preacher; one who addresses an assembly." The author of this Old Testament book claimed that he was "a son of David," perhaps meaning Solomon, but this was not really so. He probably claimed that simply to give greater authority to his words. Both the language and the ideas found in the book indicate that it was written around the second half of the third century B.C.

Ecclesiastes, or the Preacher, unlike Job, did not live a life of physical suffering. Nevertheless, he was still very dissatisfied with life. He saw life as short and unhappy, with death its sure end. Why get caught up in questions of good and evil at all? Why even go on living?

All in life is vanity, or worthless, the Preacher claimed, a tragic cycle of trouble. All that remained for humanity was friendship and love, which, even though they would eventually end, had value.

Ecclesiastes was not a person entirely without hope. He was a believer who detected behind the outer appearances of life a mystery beyond our understanding. He gave himself to God's will, but he was convinced that life after death was necessary because God was just. Unless there was life after death, this life *was* indeed meaningless and hardly worth the pain of living.

35

The Book of Psalms is a collection of songs
written over a long period of time.
While many psalms are for use
by a group of worshipers,
some are for private use.
Many are hymns of praise and thanksgiving to God.

The word *psalm* comes from the Greek word *psalmoi,* meaning "songs accompanied on the lyre." The Book of Psalms contains one hundred and fifty psalms meant to be sung. Like all poets, the authors wrote using images reflecting their own time and experiences. The psalms were written over a very long period of time by different poets. David's name is associated with many of them. Throughout the ages Jews and Christians have cherished the psalms and used them in worship.

In general, the psalms are prayer, addressed to God. Some are psalms of thanksgiving, by individuals or by groups. Some are hymns of praise to God. Other psalms are the heartfelt cries of suffering individuals or the prayers of a whole group of people experiencing a disaster. Still others are "wisdom" psalms that comment on the destiny of just and unjust persons. There are even more kinds of psalms, since the psalms are marvelous prayers that seem to cover the entire range of human experience.

Here is one of the best-known psalms, one that was used in public worship.

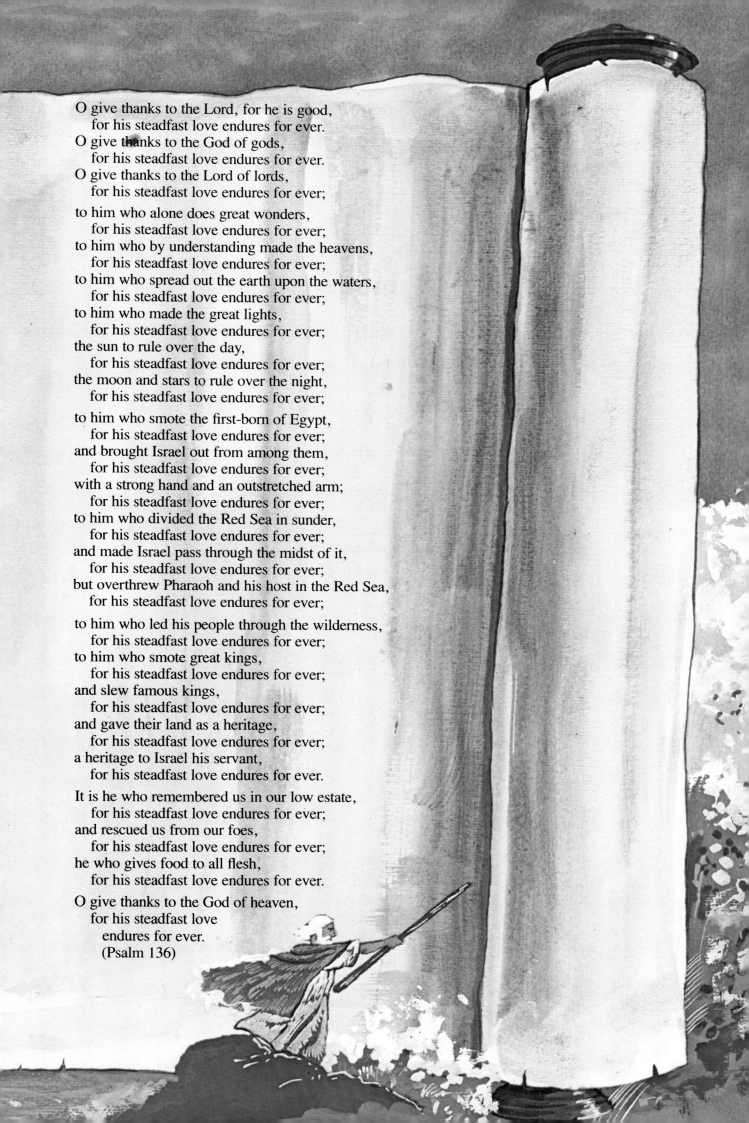

O give thanks to the Lord, for he is good,
    for his steadfast love endures for ever.
O give thanks to the God of gods,
    for his steadfast love endures for ever.
O give thanks to the Lord of lords,
    for his steadfast love endures for ever;

to him who alone does great wonders,
    for his steadfast love endures for ever;
to him who by understanding made the heavens,
    for his steadfast love endures for ever;
to him who spread out the earth upon the waters,
    for his steadfast love endures for ever;
to him who made the great lights,
    for his steadfast love endures for ever;
the sun to rule over the day,
    for his steadfast love endures for ever;
the moon and stars to rule over the night,
    for his steadfast love endures for ever;

to him who smote the first-born of Egypt,
    for his steadfast love endures for ever;
and brought Israel out from among them,
    for his steadfast love endures for ever;
with a strong hand and an outstretched arm;
    for his steadfast love endures for ever;
to him who divided the Red Sea in sunder,
    for his steadfast love endures for ever;
and made Israel pass through the midst of it,
    for his steadfast love endures for ever;
but overthrew Pharaoh and his host in the Red Sea,
    for his steadfast love endures for ever;

to him who led his people through the wilderness,
    for his steadfast love endures for ever;
to him who smote great kings,
    for his steadfast love endures for ever;
and slew famous kings,
    for his steadfast love endures for ever;
and gave their land as a heritage,
    for his steadfast love endures for ever;
a heritage to Israel his servant,
    for his steadfast love endures for ever.

It is he who remembered us in our low estate,
    for his steadfast love endures for ever;
and rescued us from our foes,
    for his steadfast love endures for ever;
he who gives food to all flesh,
    for his steadfast love endures for ever.

O give thanks to the God of heaven,
    for his steadfast love
      endures for ever.
      (Psalm 136)

36 Some psalms are cries to God, asking for help in time of sorrow or trouble.

The psalms are the prayers through which the Jews expressed their deepest feelings about their relationship with God. In them, believers praise God, give thanks to God, ask for help, and cry out in sorrow or trouble. Some of the psalms were sung by a group of worshipers publicly in the Temple; others were more likely recited in private. So there are collective psalms and individual psalms. In the preceding chapter there was an example of a public liturgical psalm. Here are two very personal, heartfelt psalms in which God's help is sought—Psalms 27 and 130.

In the first of these psalms, the believer, surrounded on all sides with enemies, is afraid; yet through all these difficulties the believer realizes that God is there to help and support. The believer's fears and worries are expressed in the middle of the prayer, with expressions of faith and confidence in God at the beginning and the end of the psalm.

In the second of these psalms, the believer prays to be delivered not from external enemies but rather from personal guilt. The person asks God's pardon in a way that reveals a close personal relationship with God. The believer, realizing that sin has offended God, in the psalm asks God to forget the sin and thereby remove the obstacle to their continued friendship.

This psalm has been particularly loved by Christians over the years. It has long been prayed as a memorial to the dead.

The Lord is my light and my salvation;
    whom shall I fear?
The Lord is the stronghold of my life;
    of whom shall I be afraid?
When evildoers assail me,
    uttering slanders against me,
my adversaries and foes,
    they shall stumble and fall.
Though a host encamp against me,
    my heart shall not fear;
though war arise against me,
    yet I will be confident.
One thing have I asked of the Lord,
    that will I seek after;
that I may dwell in the house of the Lord
    all the days of my life,
to behold the beauty of the Lord,
    and to inquire in his temple.
For he will hide me in his shelter in
    the day of trouble;
he will conceal me under the cover of his tent,
    he will set me high upon a rock.
And now my head shall be lifted up
    above my enemies round about me;
and I will offer in his tent
    sacrifices with shouts of joy;
I will sing and make melody to the Lord.
Hear, O Lord, when I cry aloud,
    be gracious to me and answer me!

Thou hast said, "Seek ye my face."
  My heart says to thee,
"Thy face, Lord, do I seek."
  Hide not thy face from me.
Turn not thy servant away in anger,
  thou who hast been my help.
Cast me not off, forsake me not,
  O God of my salvation!
For my father and my mother have forsaken me,
  but the Lord will take me up.
Teach me thy way, O Lord;
  and lead me on a level path
  because of my enemies.
Give me not up to the will of my adversaries;
  for false witnesses have risen against me,
  and they breathe out violence.
I believe that I shall see the goodness of the Lord
  in the land of the living!
Wait for the Lord;
  be strong, and let your heart take courage;
  yea, wait for the Lord!   (Psalm 27)

Out of the depths I cry to thee, O Lord!
  Lord, hear my voice!
Let thy ears be attentive
  to the voice of my supplications!

If thou, O Lord, shouldst mark iniquities,
  Lord, who could stand?
But there is forgiveness with thee,
  that thou mayest be feared.

I wait for the Lord, my soul waits,
  and in his word I hope;
my soul waits for the Lord
  more than watchmen for the morning,
  more than watchmen for the morning.

O Israel, hope in the Lord!
  For with the Lord there is steadfast love,
  and with him is plenteous redemption,
And he will redeem Israel
  from all his iniquities.   (Psalm 130)

37 When he died in 323 B.C.,
Alexander the Great was
the most powerful ruler
in the Mediterranean area.

Italy and Rome

Between 400 and 300 B.C. the land that is now Italy was inhabited by a number of different peoples. The city of Rome controlled a sizable territory around the city called Latium. An invasion by the Gauls in 390 B.C. resulted in the capture and burning of Rome. In spite of this disaster, Rome recovered quickly and was soon at war again. By 272 B.C. Rome had succeeded in unifying the entire Italian peninsula. Soon after that, Rome began its wars with Carthage, a powerful city in northern Africa.

Greece

After the Greeks won great victories over the Persians at Marathon, Salamis, and Plataea early in the fifth century B.C., the Persian emperors Darius I and Xerxes had to give up trying to dominate. The age when the city of Athens was supreme—the great Age of Pericles—began then. (Pictured on the map is the Acropolis, the hill that was the center of ancient Athens. The main structure was a temple called the Parthenon.) Later, the Peloponnesian Wars broke out among the Greek city states themselves (431-404 B.C.). They ended with the defeat of Athens at Aegospotami (404 B.C.) and the rise of Sparta's dominance in Greece (404-371 B.C.). Other civil wars led to the dominance of Thebes over the district of Boeotia (371-362 B.C.). In the meantime, the kingdom of Macedonia, located to the north of the Greek city-states, was growing into a great power that threatened the liberty of the Greeks. The Greeks spent much time quarreling among themselves and little time uniting themselves against a common enemy.

Macedonia

The Macedonians were Greek in origin, although they had lived on the edge of Greek culture and did not get involved in the quarrels among the Greek city-states. They gradually absorbed the best in Hellenic (Greek) culture and eventually spread it to the east, even as far as to India. From his capital at Pella, the Macedonian King Philip II began to gain dominance over Greece itself; through a treaty of peace with Athens and its allies in 346 B.C., he took control of Thessaly and Phocis (with its famous shrine of the oracle at Delphi). Ten years later Philip was assassinated. His son, Alexander III, succeeded him. This Macedonian king would be called Alexander "the Great."

The Empire of Alexander the Great

Alexander the Great brought together all the Greek city-states that he controlled in order to destroy forever the threat from the immense Persian Empire. After first defeating his main Greek rival, the city-state of Thebes, in 334 B.C., at age twenty-two, Alexander embarked with an army of 32,000 infantrymen, 5,000 cavalrymen, and 160 ships. He landed at Troas in Asia Minor and won a vic-

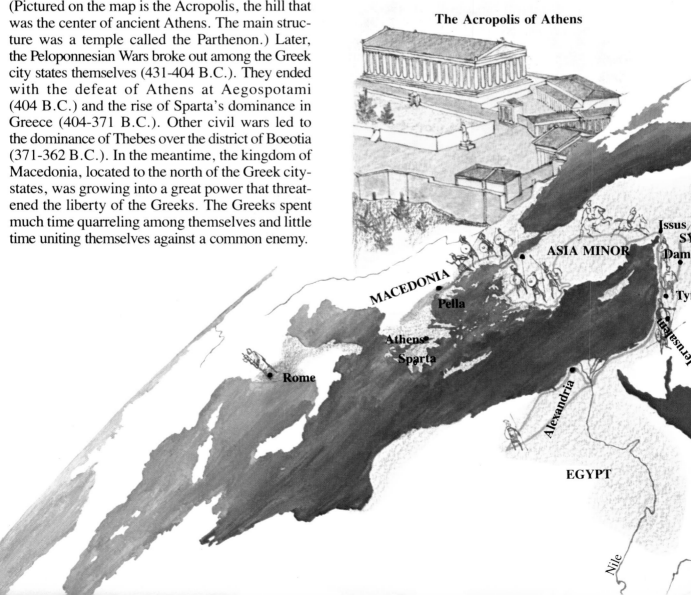

The Acropolis of Athens

tory at the Granicus River. At Issus, on the border of Asia Minor and Syria, he defeated a Persian army commanded by King Darius III himself. Darius retreated into Mesopotamia to reorganize his forces. Instead of pursuing him, Alexander turned south to take charge of Syria and Phoenicia. After a siege, he captured Tyre, the city long considered unconquerable.

On his way to Egypt, according to the Jewish historian Flavius Josephus, Alexander visited Jerusalem, where he was received by the high priest and offered sacrifices in the Temple. He promised some extra favors to the Jewish people.

He conquered Egypt, where he was greeted as a liberator from the Persians. Then he headed east again and crossed the Tigris and the Euphrates. He defeated Darius in 331 B.C. at Gaugamela. Alexander the Great went on to conquer Susa, Persepolis, and Ecbatana. He even reached India's borders. Returning to Babylon in 323 B.C., he was stricken with fever and died at age thirty-two.

Macedonia

Greek City-States

The Campaign of Alexander

Empire of Alexander

Rome

Alexander

BACTRIA

INDIA

Indus

Rages

Ecbatana

Gaugamela

Susa

gris

MESOPOTAMIA

Persepolis

uphrates

Babylon

38 Alexander the Great spread the language and customs of Greece throughout his large empire. The city of Alexandria in Egypt was a center of Greek culture.

Alexander the Great founded Alexandria, a Greek city that was built on Egyptian soil. This was the beginning of a very important new movement: the transplanting of Greek civilization into the eastern world and its blending with the ancient eastern cultures of Syria, Phoenicia, Babylonia, and Persia.

The Persian empire had been a collection of different peoples, each of which tended to maintain its own distinct way of life. Alexander, however, wanted to create a unified culture throughout his empire. His plan, continued by his successors, succeeded for the most part and gave birth to that broad Greek culture that has been called "Hellenistic," to set it apart from the classical Greek culture of the fifth century B.C.

Spread by the soldiers and sailors of the conquering Macedonians, the Greek language was soon used throughout the empire. The upper classes everywhere quickly learned it, and it was used in business affairs. Eventually Greek was the major language in both Egypt and all the East.

The government of the city of Alexandria was modeled on the democratic systems of the Greek city-states. In addition to Alexandria, other new cities were established around the empire; some

of them also were named after Alexander the Great. At the same time, older cities were reorganized along the lines of the prevailing new, Hellenistic ideas. These Hellenistic ideas survived even when Alexander's empire was divided up by his successors.

Even religion was influenced by Hellenism. Some of the ancient gods of the Egyptians became identified with some of the Greek gods. The Greek gods also were mixed with local gods in many other places throughout the East. This process of fusing, or blending, different religions into one another is called *syncretism*.

A symbol of the dominance of the new Hellenistic ideas was the setting up of libraries. The most famous of all these libraries was at Alexandria itself; for centuries it very effectively both preserved Greek literature and spread it abroad. Other Hellenistic institutions in Alexandria were the gymnasium, the place where athletic events were held, and the theater, which the Greeks introduced in the East.

Alexander even wanted to fuse races. He favored and promoted marriages between his Macedonian officers and the daughters of the local leaders in the lands he conquered. He himself married Roxane, a Bactrian princess, and later Statira, the daughter of Darius III.

A fusion of races, however, would have taken many years. It did not happen because Alexander's empire became divided up by his leading generals shortly after his death. These generals, called *diadochoi,* or successors, took over sections of the empire, and later they fought civil wars among themselves for control of territory.

The Wars of the Diadochoi went on for nearly forty years. Finally, following the Battle of Corupedion in Lydia in 281 B.C., the former empire of Alexander the Great was divided into three parts: 1) Macedonia, including Greece, under Demetrius Poliorcetes, son of Alexander's general Antigonus; 2) the kingdom of the Seleucids, which included northern Syria, Asia Minor, Mesopotamia, and Persia; Alexander's general Seleucus I was its ruler; and 3) the kingdom of the Ptolemies, which included Egypt, Libya, Palestine, Phoenicia and Cyprus; this kingdom was under Ptolemy II, son of Alexander's able general Ptolemy Soter.

39 Because many Jews
of the Diaspora
no longer spoke Hebrew,
about 250 B.C. the Scriptures
were translated into Greek.
This translation is called
the Septuagint.

The work of translating these books into Greek took place around the middle of the third century B.C., that is, around 250 B.C. The other biblical books were translated later, over the course of about a century. By 100 B.C. all the books of the Old Testament had been translated into Greek and were in wide use among the Jewish communities in which Greek was spoken.

Starting with its founding in 332 B.C., Alexandria was the home of a fair number of prosperous Jews. These Alexandrian Jews kept in close touch with Jerusalem and remained faithful to their religion. However, they were also in continuous contact with the surrounding Greek culture; they did not try to limit their contacts to other Jews. In fact, they tried to show the pagans around them the superiority of their own religious and moral ideas. These ideas, of course, were contained in the Bible, their collection of sacred writings. But the Bible was written in Hebrew and therefore couldn't be understood by non-Jews. And after a few generations had passed, many of the Jews in Alexandria had forgotten the language of their ancestors and spoke only Greek.

Due to these circumstances, a translation of the Scriptures into Greek became necessary. The first five books of the Bible were called the *Torah* ("Law") in Hebrew; they contained the basics of Jewish law and practice. These were the first books of the Bible to be translated into Greek; they were called the *Pentateuch*, which means "five books." Individually, the books were given the names by which we still know them today: *Genesis* ("origin"); *Exodus* (a "going out," that is, from Egypt); *Leviticus* (the book containing the Law for the Levites); *Numbers* (*arithmoi* in Greek, because it contained census data); and *Deuteronomy* (the "second Law," or the updating and renewal of the Law).

This Greek translation of the Bible became known as the Septuagint. This name came from a legend about the origin of the Bible in Greek that was told in the *Letter of Aristeus,* a book that promoted Jewish ideas. This book claimed that it was Ptolemy II Philadelphus (283-246 B.C.), the second successor of Alexander in Egypt, who decided that the Bible should be translated into Greek.

He wanted the sacred books of the Jews in the library of Alexandria. According to this account, the king got in touch with the high priest Eleazar, who sent from Jerusalem seventy-two learned Jews who were fluent in both Greek and Hebrew. These learned men were supposed to have completed the entire translation of the Old Testament into Greek in seventy-two days while confined on the island of Pharos in Alexandria's harbor. And so the name *Septuagint,* meaning "seventy," was given to the translation, after these seventy-odd translators.

The Septuagint Bible was used by the Christians from the time of the apostles. This was to be expected, because Greek was the language of the cities where Christianity was first preached and began to spread: Antioch, Thessalonica, Corinth, Ephesus. The Septuagint was also used in Rome, where the upper classes often spoke Greek, as did foreign merchants and the many foreign slaves there.

Not until the second century A.D. was the Greek Old Testament translated into Latin, the language of Rome. This translation was made into "old Latin." Since it was the translation of a translation, it had many defects. It was for this reason that later Jerome, who knew both Greek and Hebrew as well as Latin, spent seventeen years (A.D. 389 to 405) translating the Old Testament directly from Hebrew into Latin (except for Baruch, Sirach, Wisdom and Maccabees, which never existed in Hebrew). This translation of Jerome's along with a Latin translation of the New Testament made up the Latin Bible called the Vulgate (this is, "publicized" or "spread abroad"). The Vulgate was used for centuries by the Christian Church.

40 The Book of Sirach tries to show
the truth and value
of Jewish law and tradition.
The author emphasizes
the importance of friendship
and of honoring parents.

Jesus Ben Sirach, or "the son of Sirach," lived in Jerusalem around 190 B.C. During that period of time the Jewish traditions were threatened by the influence of Hellenism. Ben Sirach was a scribe who set out to show how the ancient Law of Moses and the Jewish traditions together made up a true wisdom that helped one to live a happy and productive life. Judaism, in Ben Sirach's view, did not have to take second place to any other culture or way of life.

The Book of Sirach,* which is sometimes called Ecclesiasticus, begins with these words: "Many great teachings have been given to us through the Law and the prophets and the others that followed them, on account of which we should praise Israel for instruction and wisdom" (Sirach: Prologue).

The basic idea on which everything else rests according to the Book of Sirach, is "the fear of

* This book is accepted by Roman Catholics but not by most Protestants.

the Lord," which will make one obey the word of the Lord, follow in his ways, and seek to please him.

"Those who fear the Lord will prepare their
hearts,
and will humble themselves before him.
Let us fall into the hands of the Lord,
but not into the hands of men."

(Sirach 2:17-18)

The author of this book carefully reviewed the sacred history of his people. He pointed with pride to the great persons God had raised up and the mighty signs and wonders God had accomplished through them.

His teachings covered a number of other topics; among them relationships in the family. He emphasized the duty of children to honor their father and mother, especially when their parents grow old and lose their former strength and intelligence. This kind of caring is the basis for all human community, according to the Book of Sirach.

For the Lord honored the father above the
children,
and he confirmed the right of the
mother over her sons.
Whoever honors his father atones for sins,
and whoever glorifies his mother is
like one who lays up treasure.

(Sirach 3:2-4)

Honor your father by word and deed,
   that a blessing from him may come upon
      you,
For a father's blessing strengthens the
   houses of the children,
but a mother's curse uproots their foundations.
                   (Sirach 3:8-9)

Whoever forsakes his father is like a blasphemer,
   and whoever angers his mother is cursed by
      the Lord.   (Sirach 3:16)

This devotion of children toward their parents will create a link between generations so that values can be passed on—values that make life worth living.

Parents also have serious duties towards their children. Their duty to educate their children is especially important. The Book of Sirach urges parents to be very strict with their children, rather than lenient.

He who loves his son will whip him often,
   in order that he may rejoice at the
      way he turns out.
Give him no authority in his youth,
   and do not ignore his errors.
Discipline your son and take pains with him,
   that you may not be offended by his
      shamelessness.   (Sirach 30: 1, 11, 13)

A parent has the duty to educate a child in order to prepare him or her for facing up to and coping with the problems of living.

The father may die, and yet he is not dead,
   for he has left behind him one like himself;
while alive he saw and rejoiced,
   and when he died he was not grieved.
                   (Sirach 30:4-5)

The Book of Sirach has harsh words for those women who throw aside their responsibilities as wives and mothers and selfishly devote themselves to enticing and attracting men ("Do not be ensnared by a woman's beauty." Sirach 25:21) On the other hand, however, there are words of praise for the virtuous woman:

A wife's charm delights her husband,
   and her skill puts fat on his bones.
A silent wife is a gift of the Lord,
   and there is nothing so precious as
      a disciplined soul.
A modest wife adds charm to charm,
   and no balance can weigh the value of
      a chaste soul.
Like the sun rising in the heights of the Lord,
   so is the beauty of a good wife in her
      well-ordered home.   (Sirach 26:13-16)

Some of the other teachings in the Book of Sirach are about gaining experience by travel, opening one's mind to a wide range of knowledge, being cheerful in order to live a good life, and valuing true friendship.

The contents of the Book of Sirach are like the words of a wise adult passing on to family members the fruits of long experience. Not everything that is said can necessarily be adapted to the changed world in which Ben Sirach's descendants find themselves. Customs must change when conditions change. But whatever the conditions, people should always seek truth, do good, and take responsibility for the gifts that the Lord has given them. This is a teaching that does not change.

41 After Alexander's death,
his empire was divided.
For a time Palestine
was controlled by Egypt.
Then the Seleucid dynasty
of Syria defeated Egypt.
Some of the Seleucid rulers
persecuted the Jewish religion.
The two Books
of the Maccabees tell about
persecution of the Jews
and about Jewish heroes,
especially the family
of Mattathias.

After Alexander's empire was divided up, Judea belonged to a territory known as "Lower Syria" (Coele-Syria). Lower Syria included Palestine, Phoenicia, and the southern part of Syria including Damascus. This territory was ruled by Ptolemy I, the founder of the Ptolemaic dynasty in Egypt, which ruled there until the Roman conquest in 30 B.C. The Ptolemies' capital was Alexandria.

The eastern part of Alexander's empire—which included northern Syria, Asia Minor, Mesopotamia, and Persia—was ruled by Seleucus I and his successors. The Seleucid dynasty (the family of Seleucus) ruled from Antioch, a city founded by Antiochus I (280-261 B.C.), son and successor of Seleucus I.

Lower Syria was frequently crisscrossed by armies, for both the Ptolemies of Egypt and the Seleucids of Syria were trying to take control of that area. The wars between the Seleucids and the Ptolemies continued up to the reign of Antiochus IV (175-163 B.C.). (These wars were described in a prophecy in chapter eleven of the Book of Daniel.)

Up to the year 199 B.C., Judea, along with all of Lower Syria, remained under the rule of the Ptolemies of Egypt. During this period the Jewish community in Jerusalem flourished as the one in Alexandria did. The Jews paid taxes to Alexandria, and the Ptolemies allowed the Jews to be independent and to govern themselves according to their own religious and civil laws. Then in

199 B.C. Lower Syria, including Judea, was conquered by the Seleucid ruler Antiochus III ("the Great"). The Seleucids had fought the Egyptians several times and finally succeeded in defeating them at Paneas, near the source of the Jordan river. Judea was now part of the empire of the Seleucids, and its people now paid taxes to Antioch.

During this period Roman power began to increase in the East. The Romans first defeated Hannibal and the Carthaginians in the great battle of Zama in 202 B.C., and then they went on to defeat Philip V of Macedonia at Cynoscephalae in 197 B.C. and Antiochus III at Magnesia in 189 B.C. As a result of the battle at Magnesia, the Seleucids lost Asia Minor to the Romans; they still controlled Judea.

Seleucus IV succeeded Antiochus III; after he was assassinated, his brother Antiochus IV took over. During his rule Antiochus IV greatly persecuted the Jewish religion. Because of his oppression of the Jews, a brave group of Jewish rebels, led by the Maccabees, began the fight for freedom.

The two biblical Books of Maccabees* narrate the events of this revolt against the Seleucids. The first of these books was originally written in Hebrew but was preserved only in Greek. It gives an account of the persecution of Antiochus IV, and of the consequent Jewish revolt led first by the

* These books are accepted by Roman Catholics but not by most Protestants.

elderly priest Mattathias, and then by his sons Judas, Simon, and Jonathan. The book ends with Simon's death in 134 B.C.

The second Book of Maccabees begins in the time of Seleucus IV and ends with the victory of Judas Maccabeus over the Syrian general Nicanor in 165 B.C. This second book, written in Greek in Alexandria, shows a greater religious motive in its composition than the first book. It praises the faithfulness of the Jewish martyrs and the holiness of Judas Maccabeus. It also proclaims the resurrection of the dead and recognizes that God's plan can be seen in the unhappy events of the history of God's people as well as in their victories.

42 The Syrian rulers
of the Seleucid dynasty
threatened Jewish life
by trying to force Jews
to adopt Greek customs
and religious traditions.
Some Jews, called Hellenizers,
even supported
this Greek influence.

As the second century B.C. dawned, there was trouble on the horizon for the Jewish people, due to some recent shifts in power among the empires. First, the Seleucids took Judea over from Egypt and appeared to be the major power in the East. Then, around 190 B.C., the Romans came upon the scene. Allying themselves with the Egyptians, they began to tip the balance in their own favor. The Seleucids, struggling to keep up with the expense of continual wars, began to demand more from the various territories under their rule, including Judea.

The story of these years is told in both Books of Maccabees. The second book begins with the earliest events in the story — some attempts by the Seleucids to take the Temple treasury for their own use. The Seleucids were helped in these efforts by the Hellenizers — Jews who had embraced the Greek way of life. The Hellenizers were willing to abandon the religion and traditions of their ancestors in order to come to terms with the surrounding civilization.

The story begins during the reign of Seleucus IV, who reigned over the Seleucid kingdom between 187 and 175 B.C. Supreme authority in Judea at that time belonged to the Jewish high priest. This high priest, Onias, was a pious man and respectful of the Law. He was admired by all the Jews, except for the Hellenizing Jews, who wished to get rid of him at all costs.

Even among the priests there were some Hellenizers. Their leader was a man named Simon, who was the administrator of the Temple. Unable to persuade Onias, the high priest, to accept Greek ideas and traditions, Simon left Jerusalem and went to see Apollonius of Tarsus, the governor of

Phoenicia and Lower Syria. Simon told Apollonius that the Temple treasury contained vast sums of money that were not serving any purpose or contributing to the Temple sacrifices. Apollonius reported to the Seleucid government what Simon had told him about huge sums of money in the Jerusalem Temple treasury.

The Seleucids sent a man named Heliodorus to Jerusalem to confiscate this money. Heliodorus went to the high priest Onias and told him the reason for his visit. Dismayed, Onias explained that the Temple treasury consisted only of some small deposits of money made by widows and orphans and that the amounts were much smaller than those reported by Simon. Heliodorus, however, refused to listen. Instead, he announced the day when he would return to the Temple to take the money in the treasury.

According to a legendary account stressing the holiness of the Temple, faithful Jews hurried to the Temple and prayed that the money would be kept safe. Robed in their vestments, the priests, too, prayed to be delivered from this threatened evil.

One day Heliodorus, with soldiers at his side, tried to enter the Temple. Suddenly, however, a mysterious stranger dressed in golden armor appeared mounted on a horse. He moved towards Heliodorus and the horse trampled Heliodorus with his front hooves. Two other strangers also appeared, and they beat the king's messenger. Heliodorus fell to the ground, incapable of moving. His men had to pick him up and carry him away. The Jews were saved for the moment: God had intervened to save the Temple from this profanation.

43 Corruption was found
among religious leaders.
Several persons tried to buy
the office of high priest.
One high priest even killed
a former high priest.

In spite of the failure of the mission of Heliodorus, the Hellenizing Jews did not give up. Very soon Simon made false accusations against Onias, and in Jerusalem Simon's supporters caused riots in which a number of people were killed. Finally Onias realized that he needed to defend himself against his accuser. Since the governor, Apollonius, supported Simon, the high priest decided to appeal directly to the king in Antioch.

At that very time important changes in the court at Antioch were taking place. Seleucus IV had been assassinated, and his throne had passed to his brother, Antiochus IV. The brother of Onias, Jason, went to the new king and offered him a huge sum of money in order to be named as high priest in the place of Onias. Jason offered further payments in return for permission to build a gymnasium where the athletic events typical of Greek culture could take place.

Antiochus IV eagerly agreed and accepted both of Jason's proposals, along with the bribes. Jason returned to Jerusalem as high priest to carry out his plans. King Antiochus abolished the traditional Jewish government by priests and clan chiefs and replaced it with a Greek-style city-state. Jason proceeded to have the gymnasium built. To show how far the Hellenizing Jews had gone in their efforts to copy the Greeks, the biblical writer mentions that the sons of prominent Jerusalem families had taken to wearing the wide-brimmed Greek hat. Modeled after the hat worn by the Greek god Hermes, the hat was an insult to religious Jews. Hellenization was threatening to extinguish Jewish religion, culture, and traditions.

Three years after Jason became high priest, he sent to Antioch a delegation headed by Menelaus, the brother of Simon, the ex-administrator of the Temple who had already caused so much trouble for Onias. Once again an offer was made to buy the office of high priest. This time it was Menelaus who offered the king sums of money in exchange for being named to the office himself. One betrayer was double-crossing the other! The biblical author comments at this point: "So Jason, who after supplanting his own brother was supplanted by another man, was driven as a fugitive into the land of Ammon" (2 Maccabees 4:26). (Ammon was east of the Jordan river.)

Back in Jerusalem Menelaus began his job as high priest, but he was in trouble because he was unable to come up with the payment he had promised to the king for his office. At that point the king had to go into Asia Minor to put down a revolt, and in his absence Andronicus was in charge. Menelaus tried to get on the good side of Andronicus: He removed some of the golden vessels and furnishings from the Temple and presented them as a gift to Andronicus.

The former high priest Onias was living near Antioch. When he was informed of what had happened to the Temple furnishings, he protested publicly, denouncing Menelaus. Then, at the request of Menelaus, Andronicus lured Onias from his place of refuge and had him killed. One of the great defenders of the Jewish religion and Jewish traditions had met his end.

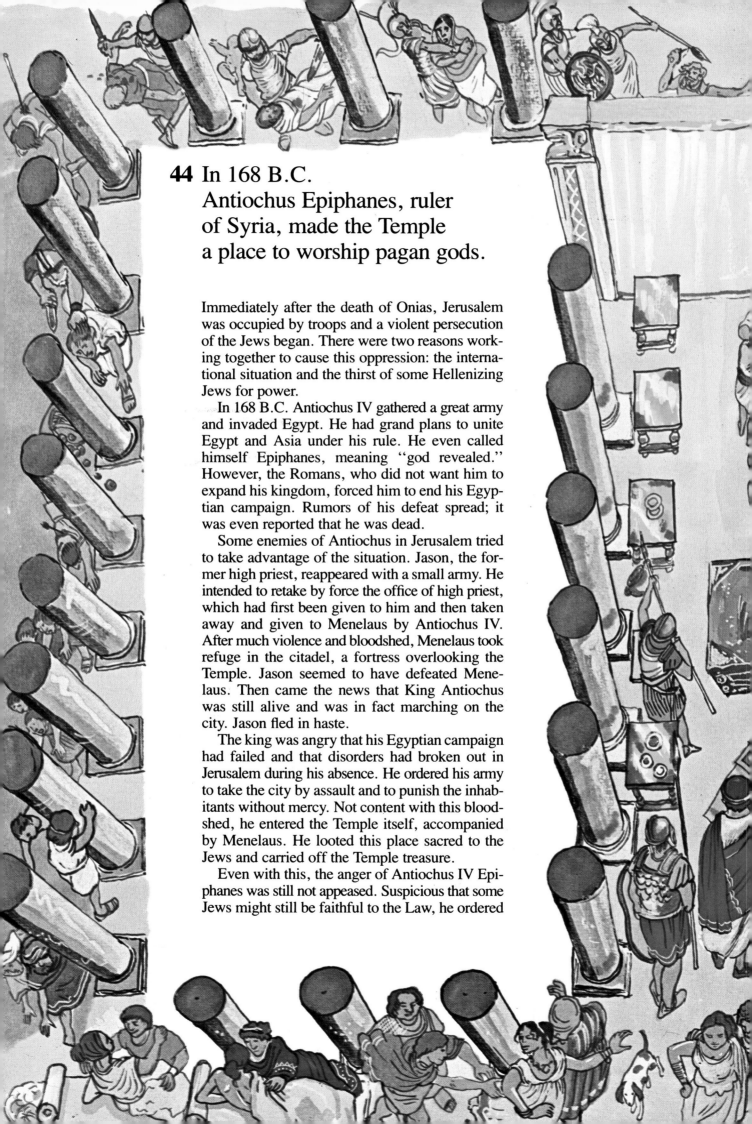

44 In 168 B.C.
Antiochus Epiphanes, ruler
of Syria, made the Temple
a place to worship pagan gods.

Immediately after the death of Onias, Jerusalem was occupied by troops and a violent persecution of the Jews began. There were two reasons working together to cause this oppression: the international situation and the thirst of some Hellenizing Jews for power.

In 168 B.C. Antiochus IV gathered a great army and invaded Egypt. He had grand plans to unite Egypt and Asia under his rule. He even called himself Epiphanes, meaning "god revealed." However, the Romans, who did not want him to expand his kingdom, forced him to end his Egyptian campaign. Rumors of his defeat spread; it was even reported that he was dead.

Some enemies of Antiochus in Jerusalem tried to take advantage of the situation. Jason, the former high priest, reappeared with a small army. He intended to retake by force the office of high priest, which had first been given to him and then taken away and given to Menelaus by Antiochus IV. After much violence and bloodshed, Menelaus took refuge in the citadel, a fortress overlooking the Temple. Jason seemed to have defeated Menelaus. Then came the news that King Antiochus was still alive and was in fact marching on the city. Jason fled in haste.

The king was angry that his Egyptian campaign had failed and that disorders had broken out in Jerusalem during his absence. He ordered his army to take the city by assault and to punish the inhabitants without mercy. Not content with this bloodshed, he entered the Temple itself, accompanied by Menelaus. He looted this place sacred to the Jews and carried off the Temple treasure.

Even with this, the anger of Antiochus IV Epiphanes was still not appeased. Suspicious that some Jews might still be faithful to the Law, he ordered a forced Hellenization of the country. He left a military force headed by a man named Apollonius and two other officials, Philip the Phrygian in Jerusalem and Andronicus in Samaria, to carry out these orders. (The Samaritans, who had become unfriendly toward the Jews at the time of the rebuilding of the Temple, had grown farther and farther away from the Jewish religion. They made no real protest when a temple in honor of the chief Greek god, Zeus, was erected on their holy mountain, Mount Gerizim.)

In Jerusalem, the Temple was rededicated to Zeus, and on the Altar of Holocausts offerings were made to the pagan gods. These horrible events took place on December 8, 167 B.C. — a date the Jews would long remember, the date of "the abomination of desolation."

No longer was the Temple the sacred place where the living God was worshiped. Rather, it was just another pagan temple like all the others. Foreigners could go in and out, and Temple prostitutes took up residence there.

It seemed that God had forgotten his people and the promises made to their ancestors. It seemed that the words of the prophets counted for nothing. But, once again, in the midst of suffering, hope was reborn, and confidence in God's help returned. This is how the author of the second Book of Maccabees interpreted this disaster:

Now I urge those who read this book not to be depressed by such calamities, but to recognize that these punishments were designed not to destroy but to discipline our people. In fact, not to let the impious alone for long, but to punish them immediately, is a sign of great kindness. For in the case of the other nations the Lord waits patiently to punish them until they have reached the full measure of their sins; but he does not deal in this way with us, in order that he may not take vengeance on us afterward when our sins have reached their height. Therefore he never withdraws his mercy from us. Though he disciplines us with calamities, he does not forsake his own people. Let what we have said serve as a reminder.   (2 Maccabees 6:12-17)

45 Antiochus commanded Jews to forsake their religion, to worship pagan gods, and to eat pork and other food forbidden by Jewish law.

Shortly after the Temple had been plundered, King Antiochus issued yet another royal order. This one commanded the Jews not to practice their religion and required them, under the threat of a death penalty, to take part in festivals honoring Dionysus and other pagan gods. "A man could neither keep the sabbath, nor observe the feasts of his fathers, nor so much as confess himself to be a Jew" (2 Maccabees 6:6).

One of the first victims of the persecution was the scribe Eleazar, a man respected both for his learning and for his old age. The authorities tried to force him to eat pork, which Jewish Law forbade. Eleazar continued to spit it out as fast as they forced it on him, preferring death to disobedience to the Law. He wished to "leave to the young a noble example of how to die a good death willingly and nobly for the revered and holy laws" (2 Maccabees 6:28).

Another moving story was that of a Jewish mother with seven sons. When they were brought before the king for having refused to eat pork and other food forbidden by Jewish Law, they publicly declared their intention of remaining faithful at all costs to the Jewish religion and to Jewish traditions. Six of the brothers were put to death in front of their mother. All the while she sustained and encouraged them in their ordeal with loving words and by sharing her belief in a future life in which she would once more see these sons.

The words of this Jewish mother proved to be extremely important ones: They represented the first expression in Jewish writings of two basic articles of Judeo-Christian faith—the creation of the world out of nothing, and life after death.

Here is the Bible's account of the death of the mother herself:

The mother was especially admirable and worthy of honorable memory. Though she saw her seven sons perish within a single day, she bore it with good courage because of her hope in the Lord. She encouraged each of them in the language of their fathers. Filled with a noble spirit, she fired her woman's reasoning with a man's courage, and said to them, "I do not know how you came into being in my womb. It was not I who gave you life and breath, nor I who set in order the elements within each of you. Therefore the Creator of the world, who shaped the beginning of man and devised the origin of all things, will in his mercy give life and breath back to you again, since you now forget yourselves for the sake of his laws."

Antiochus felt that he was being treated with contempt, and he was suspicious of her reproachful tone. The youngest brother being still alive, Antiochus not only appealed to him in words, but promised with oaths that he would make him rich and enviable if he would turn from the ways of his fathers. ... Since the young man would not listen to him at all, the king called the mother to him and urged her to advise the youth to save himself. After much urging on his part, she undertook to persuade her son. But, leaning close to him, she spoke in their native tongue as follows, deriding the cruel tyrant: "My son, have pity on me. I carried you nine months in my womb, and nursed you for three years, and have reared you and brought you up to this point in your life, and have taken care of you. I beseech you, my child, to look at the heaven and the earth and see everything that is in them, and recognize that God did not make them out of things that existed. Thus also mankind comes into being. Do not fear this butcher, but prove worthy of your brothers. Accept death, so that in God's mercy I may get you back again with your brothers."

While she was still speaking, the young man said, "What are you waiting for? I will not obey the king's command, but I obey the command of the law that was given to our fathers through Moses. But you, who have contrived all sorts of evil against the Hebrews, will certainly not escape the hands of God. For we are suffering because of our own sins. And if our living Lord is angry for a little while, to rebuke and discipline us, he will again be reconciled with his own servants. But you, unholy wretch, you most defiled of all men, do not be elated in vain and puffed up by uncertain hopes, when you raise your hand against the children of heaven. You have not yet escaped the judgment of the almighty, all-seeing God."

The king fell into a rage, and handled him worse that the others, being exasperated at his scorn. So he died in his integrity, putting his whole trust in the Lord.

Last of all, the mother died, after her sons.

(2 Maccabees 7:20-35, 39-41)

46 The priest Mattathias
and his five sons refused
to obey the king's orders.
One son, Judas Maccabeus,
became leader of an army of Jews
opposed to King Antiochus.

Many Jewish families fled Jerusalem during the persecutions of Antiochus. One such family was headed by the priest Mattathias. Taking his five sons—John, Simon, Judas, Eleazar, and Jonathan—he moved to his ancestral village, Modein, about twenty miles northwest of Jerusalem.

One day an officer of the king arrived in Modein to enforce the royal decrees that required the Jews to give up their religion. As a sign of their obedience, the Jews were ordered to offer sacrifices in the pagan Greek style on the village altar.

Since Mattathias was an honored leader in Modein, the king's officer asked him to set a good example for the others by performing the first sac-

rifice. "Now be the first to come and do what the king commands, as all the Gentiles and the men of Judah and those that are left in Jerusalem have done. Then you and your sons will be numbered among the friends of the king, and you and your sons will be honored with silver and gold and many gifts" (1 Maccabees 2:18).

Mattathias cried out in a loud voice, replying: "Even if all the nations that live under the rule of the king obey him, and have chosen to do his commandments, departing each one from the religion of his fathers, yet I and my sons and my brothers will live by the covenant of our fathers. Far be it from us to desert the law and the ordinances" (1 Maccabees 2:19-21).

Just then a frightened Jew hurried to the altar of the pagans to begin a sacrifice there. Mattathias was so outraged by this cowardice and betrayal that he threw himself upon the traitor and killed him. He also killed the king's officer and tore down the altar. Then he ran through the city, shouting "Let every one who is zealous for the law and supports the covenant come out with me!" (1 Maccabees 2:27).

Mattathias and his sons and his new followers then fled to the hills, leaving behind their possessions. There they learned how more than a thousand Jews had been slaughtered outside Jerusalem because they had refused to defend themselves on the Sabbath from the king's soldiers. Mattathias and his followers mourned for them, but they decided that they themselves would fight back — Sabbath or not — in order to save the people from complete destruction. Many more resisters joined them, and soon they had an army ready for guerrilla warfare — lightning-quick attacks by small, fearless bands of soldiers.

But the hour of death approached for the aged Mattathias. He gathered his sons around him and told them, "Arrogance and reproach have now become strong; it is a time of ruin and furious anger. Now, my children, show zeal for the law, and give your lives for the covenant of your fathers" (1 Maccabees 2:49-50). He went on to talk about the virtues of the Jewish patriarchs and leaders. He appointed his son Simon to take his place as the family leader, and another son, Judas Maccabeus, to lead the army. Then Mattathias died, mourned by all who had remained faithful to the Lord.

47 Judas led several victories
against the Syrian army.
Jews regained
control of the Temple,
so once again
they could worship God there.

Judas—nicknamed Maccabeus, meaning "the hammer"—was both young and brave and a genius at guerrilla warfare. His army, made up of small highly mobile groups, were very familiar with the terrain where they were fighting, and so they were able to resist large enemy armies.

Apollonius, the governor of Samaria, led the first attack against the rebels. But Judas Maccabeus struck the enemy army suddenly and with great force in the hills of Ephraim, defeating them and killing Apollonius.

A stronger army under Seron, the military governor of Syria, then moved against Judas and his men. In this army were many unfaithful Jews who had betrayed their heritage. The enemy army seemed so immense, that Judas' men wondered how they could ever fight against them. Judas, however, never lost his courage. He rekindled his

men's confidence by reminding them how much God's help counted in any battle. Then he hid his forces in the village of Beth-horon, located on top of a steep rise. At just the right moment, Judas fell upon Seron's army from above, caught it by surprise, and sent into flight those soldiers who survived the attack.

The news of his men's defeats in Judea got back to the king. He appointed Lysias to be in charge of his affairs in a large area and equipped

discouraged because of the great size of the opposing armies. Judas, however, begged his men to pray and have confidence in the Lord. "It is better for us to die in battle," he told them, "than to see the misfortunes of our nation and of the sanctuary" (1 Maccabees 3:59).

Once again Judas stationed his men on the hills, this time south of Emmaus. Gorgias attempted to surprise them with a night attack in the hills. But Judas guessed his intentions, and his men had deserted their camp before Gorgias arrived. Gorgias wandered around the hills looking for the enemy, while Judas and his men doubled back and attacked the half-empty Syrian camp. The soldiers under Nicanor were surprised, and they fled. Judas pursued them at some length, but then turned back to face Gorgias coming back down out of the hills. Seeing what had happened, Gorgias decided not to fight at all.

Lysias himself then tried to get rid of Judas. He sent another large army out against Judas, but, once again, the soldiers of the king failed to vanquish the handful of Jewish rebels. Lysias negotiated a truce: the Jews again entered Jerusalem but the Acra citadel there remained in Syrian hands.

Judas Maccabeus took advantage of this truce to purify the Temple again. The old altar that had been desecrated was dismantled, and a new one was constructed out of unhewn stones, according to the Law. The sanctuary was restored. The sacred furnishings, the golden candelabrum, and the Altar of Incense were replaced. The front of the Temple was decorated with golden crowns.

Then sacrifices to the living God were offered again on the Altar of Holocausts. Judas Maccabeus decreed that an eight-day feast of purification should henceforth be celebrated every year to commemorate the rededication of the Temple. Even today the annual Jewish festival of Hanukkah celebrates this event.

him with a large army that included even elephants in order to put down the revolt in Judea. Lysias gave Ptolemy, governor of Lower Syria, the immediate task of defeating Judas. Ptolemy had an army of forty thousand infantrymen and seven thousand cavalrymen commanded by Nicanor and another general, Gorgias. This army camped on the plain near Emmaus.

The armed groups of Judas Maccabeus assembled at Mizpah, near Jerusalem. They were very

48 Judas continued to lead
the rebellion against Syria.
A treaty of peace gave the Jews
freedom of religion,
provided they accept
the Syrian king's authority.

Before long Judas Maccabeus was fighting again, this time with the hostile neighbors of the Jews. Judas' men fought battles in Idumea, Gilead, and Galilee. The Jews won them all. What had begun as just a band of rebels had become a true religious and national movement.

Meanwhile the old king, Antiochus IV Epiphanes, had died, after having ordered that his kingdom be given to his son Antiochus V. Helping the young king to rule was the regent, Lysias.

Judas decided to take advantage of this confusion in the Seleucid kingdom to try to destroy the Syrian citadel just outside of Jerusalem. Without this stronghold the Syrians would lose military control of Palestine.

Some of the people from the citadel managed to escape and inform the king of what Judas was doing, which broke the truce made earlier. The king was furious, especially since the Jews had grown to be a very serious threat.

Lysias raised a huge army to march against Judea. The army was made up of one hundred thousand infantrymen, twenty thousand cavalrymen, and thirty-two elephants trained for war. This army met the rebels along the road at Beth-zechariah, halfway between Hebron and Jerusalem.

The elephants were drawn up in front; they had made the elephants drunk by giving them grape and mulberry wine to drink. Each elephant was surrounded by a thousand infantrymen equipped with breatplates, coats of mail, and bronze helmets. In addition, five hundred cavalrymen were assigned to follow each huge charging beast as it broke through Jewish lines. On the back of each warrior elephant was erected a wooden tower bound with straps; these towers held four armed men plus an Indian driver.

The sun shone on the shields of gold and bronze. One detachment of the king's troops was stationed on the hills, another on the plain. Judas moved his forces against this army, but in spite of an unusually brave effort, he was unable to defeat the king's forces.

Eleazar, the brother of Judas, met his death with particular bravery. Seeing an elephant equipped with royal armor, Eleazar thought it might be carrying the king himself. He fought his way through the soldiers surrounding the elephant, cutting down men on both right and left. He ran under the elephant and stabbed it through with his sword. The elephant, falling as he died, rolled over Eleazar and crushed him. Eleazar had died a hero's death.

The Jews were losing the battle. They were saved from disaster only because Lysias had to return quickly to Syria to put down a threat to his power there. Lysias needed to make peace with Judas Maccabeus so that he could turn his attention elsewhere.

In the treaty of peace that followed, the Jews were given freedom of religion, provided they recognized the overall authority of the king. And so the religious struggle begun six years before in 167 B.C. by the old priest Mattathias ended successfully under his son, Judas Maccabeus.

49 Judas asked the Romans
for help in his fight
against Syria.
Rome promised to help,
but help did not come.
Judas was killed
in battle with the Syrians.

The Jews had won their religious freedom, but they still had two big problems to deal with. First, Jerusalem, the holy city, was continually being threatened by the Syrian-occupied citadel that overlooked the Temple. Second, the office of high priest was held by persons who had bribed the Syrians in order to obtain the office.

Meanwhile, Demetrius I, a son of Seleucus IV, returned from Rome, where he had been held for many years as a hostage. He claimed for himself the kingdom that had been taken away from him by his uncle Antiochus IV and his line. The army immediately took the side of Demetrius, and Antiochus V was killed along with the second-in-command, Lysias.

Alcimus, a member of the priestly clan who favored the Greek ways of the Seleucids, asked Demetrius I to appoint him high priest. He also urged Demetrius to crush the Maccabean revolt. With the aid of a Syrian army, Alcimus was installed as high priest and governor. Although Judas and his followers won a great victory at Adasa over a force led by the Syrian general, Nicanor, Judas knew that he would not be able to hold out forever against the Seleucids. He decided to ask the Romans for help; he knew that the Romans had defeated every monarchy they encountered east or west and had forced them all to pay tribute.

The first Book of Maccabees commented on the Romans as follows: "The remaining kingdoms and islands, as many as ever opposed them, they destroyed and enslaved; but with their friends and those who rely on them they have kept friendship. They have subdued kings far and near, and as many as have heard of their fame have feared them. Those whom they wish to help and to make kings, they make kings, and those whom they wish they depose; and they have been greatly exalted" (1 Maccabees 8:11-13).

Judas Maccabeus sent a delegation to Rome to seek help and to establish a military alliance with Rome against the Greek kingdom in Syria. The Roman Senate accepted the offer of friendship from the Jews, and sent back a message inscribed on a bronze tablet, which was to be preserved as the record and memorial of the agreement reached. The message inscribed on this tablet included these words:

"May all go well with the Romans and with the nation of the Jews at sea and on land for ever, and may sword and enemy be far from them. If war comes first to Rome or to any of their allies in all their dominion, the nation of the Jews shall act as their allies wholeheartedly, as the occasion may indicate to them. And to the enemy who makes war they shall not give or supply grain, arms, money, or ships, as Rome has decided; and they shall keep their obligations without receiving any return. In the same way, if war comes first to the nation of the Jews, the Romans shall willingly act as their allies, as the occasion may indicate to them."

(1 Maccabees 8:23-27)

In spite of these grand promises, the Romans were nowhere to be seen when Judas Maccabeus was attacked soon after by Bacchides, a Seleucid general. Bacchides marched through Galilee, Samaria, and Judea and captured Jerusalem. He then pursued Judas into the hills. When Judas's men saw the great number of troops, many fled in terror. The eight hundred who remained with Judas threw themselves into the battle, but soon Judas was completely surrounded. Judas himself was killed in battle, and his army scattered.

The Hellenizers had triumphed. They soon took their revenge on those who had opposed them. The situation grew worse when famine came upon the land. Everything now seemed to be lost for the Jews.

50 Jonathan, a brother of Judas,
became leader of the Jews.
He began a dynasty
of prince-high priests.
Rivalry among Syrian leaders
for a time kept the Syrians
from trying
to conquer the Jews.

After the death of Judas Maccabeus in battle, his
followers approached his brother Jonathan and said,
"Since the death of your brother Judas there has
been no one like him to go against our enemies.
. . . So now we have chosen you today to take his
place as our ruler and leader, to fight our battle"
(1 Maccabees 9: 29-30).

So those Jews who wished to continue the
struggle against foreign rule gathered around Jon-

for two years. Jonathan's only enemies were the Hellenizing Jews, who worried that Jonathan might gain control of the office of high priest while it was vacant. This group persuaded Bacchides to try once more to get rid of the Maccabeans, but again he failed. Gradually all of Judea came to accept Jonathan as supreme leader in religious as well as in civil and military affairs.

Meanwhile the international situation was changing greatly. In Syria, a man named Alexander Balas claimed the Seleucid throne still occupied by Demetrius I. As soon as he made this claim, the Roman Senate as well as Ptolemy VI of Egypt recognized his right to the throne. Egypt even gave him their fleet to use.

A struggle for power followed. Because of its geographical location, Palestine became involved. The two contending kings—Demetrius I and his challenger Alexander Balas—both began to try to win Jonathan's favor. Each now wanted him as an ally. Demetrius called Jonathan a friend of the Seleucids and turned over to him the Jewish hostages who had been kept in the citadel. Alexander wrote to Jonathan calling him "brother" and "friend," offering him the high priesthood and even giving him the right to wear the royal purple and the gold crown of a prince. Jonathan accepted these honors and began a dynasty of prince-high priests.

The old king Demetrius I was hemmed in. From the north he was attacked by the kings of Pergamum and Cappadocia, and from the south by Alexander Balas and Ptolemy VI of Egypt. Demetrius was finally defeated in a decisive battle, and Alexander Balas became the sole king of Syria and Babylonia—the Seleucid realms.

Following Alexander's victory, Jonathan was granted other titles of honor and was said to be among the "principal friends of the king." He was also named general and governor of the province.

At this point Jonathan was practically an independent ruler, expecially since Alexander Balas, in spite of his victories, turned out to be an incompetent ruler. Soon the son of the defeated Demetrius I was rising up to try to retake the kingdom. Jonathan continued to favor Alexander. Even though Alexander was eventually defeated, Jonathan still managed to remain on good terms with the victor, who became Demetrius II. Jonathan also renewed the Jewish alliance with Rome and worked on the fortifications of Jerusalem.

Eventually Jonathan fell into a trap set by a man named Trypho, an ambitious Syrian army commander. Trypho falsely professed friendship for Jonathan but then turned on him and took him prisoner. Believing Jonathan dead, the Jews once again mourned for a fallen leader.

athan, living in the hills between Hebron and the Dead Sea. The general Bacchides went to look for the Maccabeans, but they escaped him and swam to safety across the Jordan river. At that point, Bacchides decided to stop the fighting and instead to build forts and strongholds from which he could control Judea.

After the high priest Alcimus died, Bacchides returned to the court at Antioch. Judea was at peace

51

In 142 B.C. the Syrians
recognized Simon,
the last living brother of Judas,
as governor of the Jews.
Now the Jews had peace
and independence.

Of the five sons of Mattathias, there now remained only Simon. He gathered together the people and said:

"You yourselves know what great things I and my brothers and the house of my father have done for the laws and the sanctuary; you know also the wars and the difficulties which we have seen. By reason of this all my brothers have perished for the sake of Israel, and I alone am left. And now, far be it from me to spare my life in any time of distress, for I am not better than my brothers. But I will avenge my nation and the sanctuary and your wives and children, for all the nations have gathered together out of hatred to destroy us."

(1 Maccabees 13:3-6)

The people responded to Simon enthusiastically:

"You are our leader in place of Judas and Jonathan your brother. Fight our battles, and all that you say to us we will do."

(1 Maccabees 13:8-9)

Simon then gathered together all able-bodied men for the army, and they hurried to complete the work on the walls and fortifications of Jerusalem. Then Simon and his forces moved against the army of Trypho. To avoid

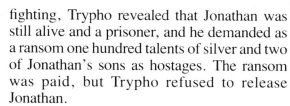

fighting, Trypho revealed that Jonathan was still alive and a prisoner, and he demanded as a ransom one hundred talents of silver and two of Jonathan's sons as hostages. The ransom was paid, but Trypho refused to release Jonathan.

Trypho next tried to invade Judea, but his advance was stopped by a sudden snowstorm. He had Jonathan killed and then retreated towards Antioch. Simon recovered the body of his brother Jonathan and had a large tomb built for him in Modein, their hometown.

At Antioch, Trypho succeeded in getting control of the kingdom of the young Antiochus VI, so Simon decided to support the rightful ruler, Demetrius II. Demetrius was pleased by this and recognized Simon as high priest and governor. He also said that the Jews did not have to pay the annual tribute and taxes.

So "the yoke of the Gentiles was removed from Israel, and the people began to write in their documents and contracts. 'In the first year of Simon the great high priest and commander and leader of the Jews' " (1 Maccabees 13:41). This was in 142 B.C. Many towns in Judea were rebuilt; and, most important, Simon was finally able to reconquer the citadel from which the Syrians had for so long threatened Jerusalem. Simon began to mint Judean coins. Judea was now independent.

Simon also renewed his alliance with Rome, sending ambassadors with gifts. The Jewish people had some bronze tablets inscribed with the deeds of Simon, his brothers, and his father. Simon was now king in everything but name.

He had to undergo one final clash with the Seleucids when a messenger of Antiochus VII arrived to deliver an ultimatum to him to withdraw from Joppa, Gazara, and the citadel. This royal envoy was amazed at the splendor of Simon's court. Simon proudly replied to the envoy, saying, "We have neither taken foreign land nor seized foreign property, but only the inheritance of our fathers, which at one time had been unjustly taken by our enemies" (1 Maccabees 15:33). A battle followed, and the Jews, led by Simon and his sons, were victorious. Eventually Simon was murdered, but his son John carried on his line.

52
Besides telling the story
of the struggles for freedom,
the two Books of the Maccabees
express faith
in the resurrection of the dead.

Besides the history in the two Books of Maccabees, there are also religious teachings. One such teaching is that God's Chosen People need to do more than just survive; they need to hold onto their beliefs and traditions.

The Jews fought to be free from foreign rule so that no one would stop them from freely practicing their religion. They also fought for freedom from others so that they would not be contaminated by other cultures, which were pagan.

Two other religious teachings in the Books of Maccabees are brought out in some of the stories told in these books.

In the course of one of the battles with the Seleucids, some of the Jews fell on the battlefield. When other Jews went to bury their comrades, they discovered that underneath their tunics the dead wore amulets and other pagan objects forbidden to Jews. "And it became clear to all that this was why these men had fallen" (2 Maccabees 12:40). Their deaths were interpreted as a divine punishment.

The survivors prayed that these sins committed by the dead might be pardoned. Judas Maccabeus took up a collection to send back to Jerusalem so that a sacrifice offered in penance could be made in the Temple. Probably at the time the battle took place such a sacrifice was understood as being offered for the survivors so that the sins of their fallen comrades would not also be blamed on them. However, the author, who wrote the account of the incident some time after it had occurred, taught that the lesson of such a sacrifice was that it was good to pray for the dead, since the dead were

destined to rise in the resurrection. The author says that if Judas "were not expecting that those who had fallen would rise again, it would have been superfluous and foolish to pray for the dead. But if he was looking to the splendid reward that is laid up for those who fall asleep in godliness, it was a holy and pious thought" (2 Maccabees 12:44-45).

The author, then, is speaking for the resurrection of the dead and the possibility of praying for the dead. Death does not completely separate the dead from the living.

In the same way, the second Book of Maccabees describes prayers that the dead can make for the living. Before a battle with the powerful Seleucid general, Nicanor, Judas Maccabeus had a vision in which he saw the dead high priest Onias. Onias had been a holy and faithful man. In Judas's vision, Onias was in heaven praying with outstretched arms for the whole Jewish people. Then Judas saw in the vision another old man, who was also praying for the people: it was the prophet Jeremiah. Pointing to Jeremiah, Onias said: "This is a man who loves the brethren and prays much for the people and the holy city" (2 Maccabees 15:14).

In the vision Jeremiah presented Judas with a golden sword and said: "Take this holy sword, a gift from God, with which you will strike down your adversaries" (2 Maccabees 15:16).

This entire incident stressed the bonds of faith and the connections between the living and the dead.

Sadducees

Pharisees

53 In the 200 years before Christ, different religious groups developed among the Jews. The Pharisees tried to keep Jewish traditions and customs. The Saduccees were more open to Greek ideas. The Essenes kept themselves separate from other Jews.

After Simon, the last of the Maccabee brothers, died, leadership in Judea passed to his son John. During the time of the Maccabees and their successors, several religious groups emerged within Judaism. Although they were different, each of these religious groups, or sects, claimed to be based on the Law of Moses as set forth in the Pentateuch.

To understand these religious groups, it is necessary to know a little about leadership in Judea after John Hyrcanus (134-104 B.C.) took over from his father Simon. The dynasty begun by John Hyrcanus was called the Hasmonean dynasty. Like his father, John was both high priest and king but did not have the title of king.

The title *king* was probably first used by the son of John Hyrcanus, whose name was Aristobulus I (104-103 B.C.). His brother and successor, Alexander Janeus, certainly bore the title of king (103-76 B.C.).

When Alexander died, his wife, Alexandra Salome, continued to rule as queen; after she died, her sons fought in a civil war between 67 and 63 B.C. The rivalry between these two brothers finally caused the Romans to intervene in the affairs of Judea in 63 B.C. The Roman leader Pompey the Great occupied Jerusalem.

When Jonathan Maccabeus in 152 B.C. accepted the office of high priest, one group of Jews disapproved so strongly that they separated themselves from the rest of the Jews. They did not believe that the political leader should also be the religious leader.

This group, known as the *Essenes*, lived in their own communities in the desert or on the shores of the Dead Sea. We have learned more about the Essenes through the discovery of the Dead Sea Scrolls in Qumran (see chapter 72). They prayed together and copied and studied the Scriptures. They did not accept the high priests of the Hasmoneans. They lived simply, gave up private property, and held everything in common, as later Christian monks and nuns would do.

Another religious group, the *Pharisees,* supported and promoted Jewish customs and traditions against the Hellenizing Jews, whom they thought were dangerous to the true religion. The Pharisees treasured not only the written Law of the Scriptures, but also the oral traditions and laws of the Jews. Leaders called *rabbis* studied Law and applied it rigorously. For example, they possessed detailed rules for the observance of the Sabbath, for ritual purification, and for the payment of tithes to the Temple.

Like the Essenes, the Pharisees disapproved of the same person being both the high priest and the governor. They believed that a king of the Jews had to be a descendant of David, while the Hasmoneans belonged to the tribe of Levi. The Pharisees were the principal teachers of the people.

The Pharisees believed in the resurrection of the dead and in a final judgment. They also taught that although there was a divine plan, only those who proved themselves by obeying all of the many religious laws and customs would be accepted by God. Because some Pharisees tried to avoid contact with people who failed to observe the laws as they did, this group was called Pharisees, meaning "the separated ones."

Yet another religious group, the *Sadducees,* were more open to Greek customs. The Sadducees accepted only the written Law of Moses in Scripture and would accept no new interpretations of that Law. They were suspicious of the increasing authority given by the Pharisees to oral law. They did not believe in the resurrection of the dead. They favored the Hasmonean rulers, and later advised cooperation with the Roman authorities in order to avoid conflict and ruin.

The main work of the *scribes* was to copy by hand the scrolls containing the Scriptures. The scribes also interpreted or explained the meaning of the Scriptures.

Scribes

Essenes

54 The northern Jewish kingdom
came to an end in 721 B.C.
After Israel fell, the people there,
called Samaritans,
married non-Jewish neighbors
and worshiped the gods
of their non-Jewish neighbors.
Other Jews considered
the Samaritans to be foreigners
and not Jews at all.
Jews and Samaritans
became very unfriendly
toward each other.

The people called the Samaritans took their name from the city of Samaria, the capital of the kingdom of Israel after its separation from the kingdom of Judah. The Samaritans began as a specific group of people after the fall of the kingdom of Israel to the Assyrians in 721 B.C. At that time the Assyrians deported the leading citizens of the kingdom of Israel, leaving only shepherds or farmers, who were unlikely to rebel against Assyrian rule.

In accord with their general policy of uprooting and transplanting subject peoples, the Assyrians then brought into Samaria subjects from Babylonia and from other cities in Syria that had been defeated. These newcomers introduced the worship of their own gods but they also began to worship Yahweh, the God still worshiped by some of the remaining Israelites. For the new pagan inhabitants, however, the Lord God Yahweh was just another god, the god of the Israelites.

Over the years, the people who lived in what was now the territory of Samaria mixed their religions together. The populations became mixed also. The Israelites married among the newcomers, and vice versa.

Later, in 538 B.C., as we have seen, Cyrus the Great gave the Jewish exiles in Babylonia permission to return to Jerusalem, to rebuild the Temple, and to restore the worship of Yahweh—all under overall Persian rule. At that time, the Samaritans, pointing out that they too were worshipers of Yahweh, wanted to unite with the Jews. However, the Jewish authorities rejected the Samaritans, because they wanted to maintain the purity of their religion and race. They saw the Samaritans not as fellow Jews but as foreigners. From that time on, the Jews and the Samaritans were very unfriendly toward each other.

About a century later, when Ezra and Nehemiah were reorganizing and renewing the Jewish community according to the book of Deuteronomy, the Jews became very aware of Deuteronomy's rule against mixed marriages, that is, against Jews' marrying non-Jewish local inhabitants. A grandson of the high priest in Jerusalem had married a daughter of Sanballat, the governor of Samaria. When he refused to divorce this wife, he was banished by Nehemiah and went to live among the Samaritans. Through him and through other priests from Jerusalem, the Samaritans' worship was purified of some of its pagan practices. Probably around this time the Samaritans began to base their religion on a version of the Pentateuch, written in a special alphabet of their own.

Around 300 B.C. the Samaritans built a temple of their own on Mount Gerizim. They considered this the only proper place to offer sacrifice. This temple was destroyed in 128 B.C. by John Hyrcanus. In 108 B.C. he leveled the city of Samaria to the ground. Naturally this made the Samaritans hate the Jews even more.

There remains today near Nablus (near the ancient city of Shechem) a small group of people descended from the ancient Samaritans. They are still faithful to their ancient traditions.

55 The Book of Daniel, written
to encourage persecuted Jews,
contains many stories
about Jews in Babylon.
One story tells of four youths
who kept Jewish dietary laws,
even in the king's palace.

The Book of Daniel was put together around 167 B.C., during the terrible persecutions of Antiochus IV Epiphanes, who tried to stamp out the Jewish religion. It was written to strengthen and comfort the Jewish people in their suffering.

The book gets its name from its hero, a young man named Daniel. Its author is unknown. The first part of the book contains stories about Daniel, which take place during the Babylonian exile. The second part is an account of the author's mysterious visions.

The various stories in the first part all aim at teaching the Jews how to remain faithful to the Law of God and reminding them how God never abandons the truly faithful. The time framework of these stories is difficult to understand. In the book, even though the years are passing, Daniel and his companions always seem to be as young as ever. However, what is most important in the stories does come through clearly: encouragement to imitate this man Daniel both in wisdom and in strength of character.

The first story about Daniel takes place in the court of King Nebuchadnezzar, the Chaldean king of Babylonia, who deported many of the Jewish people to Babylonia in 587 B.C. Nebuchadnezzar decided to select some boys from noble families to go through three years of instruction in the language, literature, and wisdom of the Chaldeans. These young men would then become scribes in the royal court.

Among the Jewish youths chosen for this kind of education were Daniel, Hananiah, Azariah, and Mishael. Because these four youths wished to remain faithful to their own religion, to the Law of God, and to the traditions of their own people, their situation in the king's palace was not easy. For example, their religion prohibited them from eating certain types of meat, so they asked that they be fed only vegetables. Besides annoying the royal cooks, this proposal frightened the steward placed in charge of them. He feared what would happen if the king noticed that some of his charges were in poorer condition than others.

Daniel proposed a solution, saying, "Test your servants for ten days; let us be given vegetables to eat and water to drink. Then let our appearance and the appearance of the youths who eat the king's rich food be observed by you, and according to what you see, deal with your servants" (Daniel 1:12-13).

The steward agreed to this test, and after ten days he saw that the four Jewish youths looked better and fatter than the others who were eating the king's food. In this way, Daniel and his companions were able to live at the court of the king without violating the Law of God.

The four Jewish youths were so successful in their studies that Nebuchadnezzar found none to compare with Daniel, Hananiah, Azariah, and Mishael. These four knew much more than all the others.

56 One story tells how
Daniel saved Susanna.
Though she was innocent,
through the plot of two evil men
Susanna had been found
guilty of adultery.

Another story in the Book of Daniel, set in the Exile, is found in Roman Catholic Bibles, but not in Protestant Bibles.

Many of the Jews in Babylonia lived in small communities with their own elders acting as "judges" of the people. Joakim was one particularly wise and able Jew living there. Highly respected by his people, he had married Susanna, a woman known for both her beauty and her goodness.

Two elders who were judges of the people were not as good as they appeared; underneath they were really very wicked. Often they visited the house of Joakim, and both of them had become very interested in Susanna.

Susanna often bathed in an enclosed inner garden. One day the two elders who desired her hid in her garden and suddenly confronted her as she was preparing for her bath. They threatened her: "Look, the garden doors are shut, no one sees us, and we are in love with you; so give your consent, and lie with us. If you refuse, we will testify against you that a young man was with you" (Daniel 13:20-21).

Susanna feared that she was lost. If she gave in to the two elders, she would be guilty in God's eyes. And if she refused to give in, she would be condemned before everyone by the two respected elders. Susanna wept bitterly: "I am hemmed in on every side. . . . I choose not to do it and to fall into your hands rather than to sin in the sight of the Lord" (Daniel 13:22, 23).

The elders then cried out and quickly opened the doors to the garden. They claimed they had mistakenly been shut into the garden while strolling there, and while inside, they had surprised Susanna in a lover's meeting with a young man who had then fled.

Since they were elders and judges of the people, their story was believed. Susanna was convicted of adultery, and, according to the Law, was condemned to death. While she was being taken to the place of execution, Susanna cried out in a loud voice: "O eternal God, . . . who art aware of all things before they come to be, thou knowest that these men have borne false witness against me. And now I am to die! Yet I have done none of the things that they have wickedly invented against me!" (Daniel 13:42-43).

Although the people pitied her, they did not believe her and they remained silent. At that moment, a young man cried out. "I am innocent of the blood of this woman!" (Daniel 13-46)

The young man was Daniel, who was already known for his goodness and wisdom. He scolded the people for having allowed Susanna to be condemned without really gathering all the facts. The people agreed to let Daniel reexamine the case.

First, Daniel asked that the two elders be separated. Then he had them called back one at a time in order to see if their stories agreed. He asked each of them in turn under which of the trees of the garden the supposed misdeed of Susanna with the young man had taken place. Unable to consult with each other about the answer, one elder said he had seen Susanna under an evergreen oak, which was a very large tree, and the other claimed it was a mastic tree, a very small tree. There could be no doubt but that the two elders had lied. All the people then praised God that the innocent Susanna had been saved.

The writer of this story wanted to teach the persecuted Jews not to fear slander or unjust trials on made-up charges. God still recognized the innocence of his true followers and knew how to defend them.

57 In another story,
Daniel interpreted
a dream of Nebuchadnezzar,
king of Babylonia,
and foretold the end
of Babylonian power.

Daniel became well known and influential among the Babylonians because he had been able to interpret the dream of the king, Nebuchadnezzar.

Nebuchadnezzar felt very troubled one morning when he awoke because he had had a disturbing dream. He called together all his wise men and magicians and said to them:

"I'm worried about a dream I've had. I want to know what it means."

They answered the king in Aramaic, "May Your Majesty live forever! Tell us your dream, and we will explain it to you."

The king said to them, "I have made up my mind that you must tell me the dream and then tell me what it means. If you can't, I'll have you torn limb from limb and make your houses a pile of ruins. But if you can tell me both the dream and its meaning, I will reward you with gifts and great honor. Now, then, tell me what the dream was and what it means."

(Daniel 2:3-6 TEV)

The wise men and magicians were dismayed at the king's command. They replied that it would be impossible to tell the dream the king had had—only a god could do anything like that. Angered, Nebuchadnezzar condemned to death all the wise men and magicians in his entire realm.

Then Daniel asked to be taken in to see Nebuchadnezzar. He told the king:

"Your Majesty, there is no wizard, magician, fortuneteller, or astrologer who can tell you that. But there is a God in heaven, who reveals mysteries. He has informed Your Majesty what will happen in the future. Now I will tell you the dream, the vision you had while you were asleep. . . .

Your Majesty, in your vision you saw standing before you a giant statue, bright and shining, and terrifying to look at. Its head was made of the finest gold; its chest and arms were made of silver; its waist and hips of bronze, its legs of iron, and its feet partly of iron and partly of clay. While you were looking at it, a great stone broke loose from a cliff without anyone touching it, struck the iron and clay feet of the statue, and shattered them. At once the iron, clay, bronze, silver, and gold crumbled and became like the dust on a threshing place in summer. The wind carried it all away, leaving not a trace. But the stone grew to be a mountain that covered the whole earth."

(Daniel 2:27-28, 31-35, TEV)

Nebuchadnezzar was very impressed with Daniel's ability to describe the dream. The Jewish prophet then proceeded to interpret the meaning of the dream:

"Your Majesty, you are the greatest of all kings. The God of heaven has made you emperor and given you power, might, and honor. He has made you ruler of all the inhabited earth and ruler over all the animals and birds. You are the head of gold. After you there will be another empire, not as great as yours, and after that a third, an empire of bronze, which will rule the whole earth. And then there will be a fourth empire, as strong as iron, which shatters and breaks everything. And just as iron shatters everything, it will shatter and crush all the earlier empires. You also saw that the feet and the toes were partly clay and partly iron. This means that it will be a divided empire. It will have something of the strength of iron, because there was iron mixed with the clay. . . . You also saw that the iron was mixed with the clay. This means that the rulers of that empire will try to unite their families by intermarriage, but they will not be able to, any more than iron can mix with clay. At the time of those rulers the God of heaven will establish a kingdom that will never end. It will never be conquered, but will completely destroy all those empires and then last forever."   (Daniel 2:37-41, 43-44 TEV)

The king marveled at Daniel's interpretation. He praised Daniel and the God of Daniel, who had the power to reveal the future. He loaded the prophet with honors.

With this story the author wanted to demonstrate that the end of the Babylonian rule had been foretold. Pagan kingdoms would succeed one another, each one less splendid but more cruel than the previous one until the kingdom of iron (or Hellenistic kingdom) arrived. (That was the one in which the author lived.) Finally, however, God would get rid of every other reign and power and would establish his own reign and power.

58
The story of three Jews
in the fiery furnace
shows God's protection
for those who refused
to worship idols.

Perhaps the best-known story in the Book of Daniel is the one about the three young companions of Daniel who together with Daniel were educated to be court scribes. In this story, King Nebuchadnezzar had fashioned an enormous golden statue. For the day of the statue's dedication, he ordered to Babylon all the officials from all the provinces of his empire. When everyone had assembled, an edict from the king was read:

"People of all nations, races, and languages! You will hear the sound of the trumpets, followed by the playing of oboes, lyres, zithers, and harps; and then all the other instruments will join in. As soon as the music starts, you are to bow down and worship the gold statue that King Nebuchadnezzar has set up. Anyone

who does not bow down and worship will immediately be thrown into a blazing furnace.''
(Daniel 3:4-6 TEV)

Everyone hurried to obey the king's order. They all fell down to worship at the sound of the music, as the king had commanded. However, the three young Jews—called Shadrach, Meshach, and Abednego by the Babylonians—did not fall down to worship, although they themselves held high office under the king in Babylon itself. Their failure to obey the king's edict was reported to him. Nebuchadnezzar was furiously angry, and he called the young men to ask for an explanation:

"Shadrach, Meshach, and Abednego, is it true that you refuse to worship my god and to bow down to the gold statue I have set up? Now

The king was beside himself with fury, and he ordered that the burning fiery furnace be stoked up until it was seven times hotter than usual. He had the three young Jews tied up and cast into the flames. The flames were so hot and they rose so high that they killed the guards who were throwing the young men in. However, the flames opened up before the three young men and did not touch them. They walked unharmed among the flames, singing songs and praising and blessing God.

The flames rose and rose. An angel of the Lord appeared in the furnace in the midst of them and kept the flames away from the three young men, creating a kind of misty wind in the middle of the fire. When the king came to look things over he saw to his immense surprise that the three young

then, as soon as you hear the sound of the trumpets, oboes, lyres, zithers, harps, and all the other instruments, bow down and worship the statue. If you do not, you will immediately be thrown into a blazing furnace. Do you think there is any god who can save you?''
(Daniel 3:14-15 TEV)

The three young men replied, saying,
"Your Majesty, we will not try to defend ourselves. If the God whom we serve is able to save us from the blazing furnace and from your power, then he will. But even if he doesn't, Your Majesty may be sure that we will not worship your god, and we will not bow down to the gold statue that you have set up.''
(Daniel 3:16-18 TEV)

Jews who had been his friends were still moving among the flames without harm. And there were four, not three, in the burning fiery furnace. The fourth seemed to be a heavenly being.

Nebuchadnezzar finally ordered the young men to be removed from the furnace. Not a hair of their heads had been harmed. They wore mantles that had not even been scorched by the fire, nor did their garments even have a burnt odor. The king then repented and stated publicly that the young men were right to risk their lives in disobeying his commands in order to observe the divine commands.

The author meant to teach that idolatry—even to escape the threat of human punishment—was always wrong.

59 In the furnace the men prayed "the canticle of the creatures."

The story of the three young men cast into the burning fiery furnace includes a beautiful prayer, a kind of "canticle of the creatures," in which God was praised and blessed for all the wonders of creation.*

Blessed art thou, O Lord, God of our fathers,
    and to be praised and highly exalted for ever;
And blessed is thy glorious, holy name
    and to be highly praised and highly exalted for ever;
Blessed art thou in the temple of thy holy glory
    and to be extolled and highly glorified for ever.
Blessed art thou, who sittest upon cherubim and lookest
        upon the deeps,
    and to be praised and highly exalted for ever.
Bless the Lord, all works of the Lord,
    sing praise to him and highly exalt him for ever.
Bless the Lord, you heavens,
    sing praise to him and highly exalt him for ever.
Bless the Lord, you angels of the Lord,
    sing praise to him and highly exalt him for ever.
Bless the Lord, all waters above the heaven,
    sing praise to him and highly exalt him for ever.
Bless the Lord, all powers,
    sing praise to him and highly exalt him for ever.
Bless the Lord, sun and moon,
    sing praise to him and highly exalt him for ever.
Bless the Lord, stars of heaven,
    sing praise to him and highly exalt him for ever.
Bless the Lord, all rain and dew,
    sing praise to him and highly exalt him for ever.
Bless the Lord, all winds,
    sing praise to him and highly exalt him for ever.
Bless the Lord, fire and heat,
    sing praise to him and highly exalt him for ever.
Bless the Lord, winter cold and summer heat,
    sing praise to him and highly exalt him for ever.
Bless the Lord, dews and snows,
    sing praise to him and highly exalt him for ever.
Bless the Lord, nights and days,
    sing praise to him and highly exalt him for ever.
Bless the Lord, light and darkness,
    sing praise to him and highly exalt him for ever.

* This passage is accepted by Roman Catholics but not by most Protestants.

Bless the Lord, ice and cold,
  sing praise to him and highly exalt him for ever.
Bless the Lord, frosts and snows,
  sing praise to him and highly exalt him for ever.
Bless the Lord, lightnings and clouds,
  sing praise to him and highly exalt him for ever.
Let the earth bless the Lord;
  let it sing praise to him and highly exalt him for ever.
Bless the Lord, mountains and hills,
  sing praise to him and highly exalt him for ever.
Bless the Lord, all things that grow on the earth,
  sing praise to him and highly exalt him for ever.
Bless the Lord, you springs,
  sing praise to him and highly exalt him for ever.
Bless the Lord, seas and rivers,
  sing praise to him and highly exalt him for ever.
Bless the Lord, you whales and all creatures that move
    in the waters,
  sing praise to him and highly exalt him for ever.
Bless the Lord, all birds of the air,
  sing praise to him and highly exalt him for ever.
Bless the Lord, all beasts and cattle,
  sing praise to him and highly exalt him for ever.
Bless the Lord, you sons of men,
  sing praise to him and highly exalt him for ever.
Bless the Lord, O Israel,
  sing praise to him and highly exalt him for ever.
Bless the Lord, spirits and souls of the righteous,
  sing praise to him and highly exalt him for ever.
Bless the Lord, you who are holy and humble in heart,
  sing praise to him and highly exalt him for ever.
Bless the Lord, Hananiah, Azariah, and Mishael,
  sing praise to him and highly exalt him for ever;
for he has rescued us from Hades and saved us from the
    hand of death,
  and delivered us from the midst of the burning fiery
    furnace;
  from the midst of the fire he has delivered us.
Give thanks to the Lord, for he is good,
  for his mercy endures for ever.
Bless him, all who worship the Lord, the God of gods,
  sing praise to him and give thanks to him,
  for his mercy endures for ever.
                    (Deuterocanonical addition to Daniel,
                      inserted between 3:23 and 3:24)

60

In one story Daniel
explained for King Belshazzar
some handwriting on the wall.
Daniel predicted
that Belshazzar
would fall from power.

Another story in the Book of Daniel concerns another dream of the king of Babylon, Nebuchadnezzar. The king said that in his dream he had seen an enormous tree in the midst of the earth, so large that its branches seemed to touch the sky. The tree, with its beautiful branches and abundant fruit, could be seen from everywhere. All the beasts of the earth found shade under it, and all the birds of the air rested in its branches.

Then suddenly a loud voice from the heavens demanded that the tree be cut down, leaving only the stump and the roots bound with chains. In the dream it almost seemed as if the stump and the roots were living, like a human heart beating. Then this heart turned into that of a beast, remaining so for seven years.

The dream was very strange. No one knew what to make of it.

Then Daniel appeared and interpreted the dream. He said it was a message from God to Nebuchadnezzar. As king he, like the immense tree, was great and powerful, but he too would be cut down. A strange affliction would make him like an animal, until he had repented of his pride and recognized that all power and might belonged to God, the Almighty. After that his kingdom would be restored to him. According to the biblical author, everything happened as the dream predicted. Some months later Nebuchadnezzar became insane. Only much later did he regain his reason and recognize

God's greatness. There is no historical record of this happening to the king. But whether or not it did is not the author's point. His lesson is that no worldly power is greater than God. Such a lesson must have comforted the first readers of the Book of Daniel, since they were being so harshly treated by the Syrian ruler, Antiochus IV.

Another of the stories in the Book of Daniel occurred during the reign of Belshazzar, said to be the successor of Nebuchadnezzar. During a great feast, Belshazzar brought in some of the sacred golden vessels that had been taken from the Temple in Jerusalem. Praising gods made of metal, wood, and stone, Belshazzar and all his court drank from these holy vessels in order to show their disrespect for the beliefs of the Jews.

Suddenly, however, a frightening thing occurred during Belshazzar's feast. A hand appeared and began writing on the wall in an unknown language. The king was terrified and immediately called for his magicians and astrologers to interpret this handwriting on the wall. No one succeeded in interpreting the writing.

Finally, at the suggestion of the queen, Daniel was summoned. Daniel was heartbroken at the sight of the defiled Temple vessels, but then he turned and read the handwriting on the wall. He explained to the king:

"You, ... Belshazzar, have not humbled your heart, ... but you have lifted up yourself against the Lord of heaven; and the vessels of his house have been brought in before you, and you and your lords, your wives, and your concubines have drunk wine from them. ...

"Then from his presence the hand was sent, and this writing was inscribed. And this is the writing that was inscribed: MENE, MENE, TEKEL, PERES. This is the interpretation of the matter: MENE, God has numbered the days of your kingdom and brought it to an end; TEKEL, you have been weighed in the balances and found wanting; PERES, your kingdom is divided and given to the Medes and the Persians."   (Daniel 5:22-28, adapted)

This prophecy was fulfilled that very night when Belshazzar was overthrown and killed.

61 The story of Daniel in the den of lions shows God's protection for those who were faithful and kept Jewish laws.

Another story in the Book of Daniel happened during the period after the Medes and the Persians had conquered Babylonia. The king in the city of Babylon itself was Darius the Mede (a ruler unknown to historians outside of this mention in the Book of Daniel). This story, like so many in Daniel, was written long after the time it was supposed to have taken place. Its main purpose is to teach a moral lesson.

During the reign of Darius, Daniel was a very important person, one of three rulers over the kingdom. When Darius decided to put Daniel in charge of the whole kingdom, the other two rulers and other officials became very jealous and wanted to see him disgraced. They decided to play on Daniel's only "weakness"—which was his constant faithfulness to the Jewish Law.

So some of them persuaded the king to issue a command condemning to death anyone who over a period of thirty days asked for anything from any god or person except the king himself.

Daniel usually prostrated himself in the direction of the Temple in Jerusalem and prayed three times a day. It was not long, therefore, before he was discovered disobeying the king's order, and he was taken before the king.

Darius liked Daniel and did not want to see him condemned; he was saddened at the accusation brought against him. However, he felt the edict he had issued could not be changed. So Daniel was taken to the lions' den. The king even said to him in parting, "May your God, whom you serve continually, deliver you" (Daniel 6:16).

Daniel was thrown in with the lions, and a huge stone was rolled over the entrance way. This stone was marked with the king's royal seal. The king

returned to his palace and refused to eat. He watched anxiously all night, wondering about the fate of Daniel.

Early the next morning the king hurried back to the lions' den. As he approached he called out: "O Daniel, servant of the living God, has your God, whom you serve continually, been able to deliver you from the lions?" (Daniel 6:20)

The king was both surprised and overjoyed when Daniel replied from inside the lions' den. "O king, live for ever! My God sent his angel and shut the lions' mouths, and they have not hurt me, because I was found blameless before him; and also before you, O king, I have done no wrong" (Daniel 6:22).

The king then ordered Daniel brought out of the lions' den, and his accusers were put there in his place. Then King Darius the Mede issued a decree to all his subjects asking that the God of Daniel be praised and feared:

"I command that throughout my empire everyone should fear and respect Daniel's God.
"He is a living God,
   and he will rule forever.
His kingdom will never be destroyed,
   and his power will never come to an end.
He saves and rescues;
   he performs wonders and miracles
   in heaven and on earth.
He saved Daniel from being killed by the
   lions." (Daniel 6:26-27 TEV)

This story has two lessons: No power is greater than the power of God, who saves those who are faithful to him. One day all the peoples of the earth, including the most powerful of rulers, will come to accept the rule of the one God of Israel.

62 Daniel's vision of four beasts
teaches that God's kingdom
is greater than
any earthly kingdom.

The first part of the Book of Daniel contains many stories about the legendary Jewish hero, Daniel. The second part is a series of Daniel's visions about the future. Writings about what God has in store for the future are called "apocalyptic" literature. The Book of Daniel is the first example of apocalyptic literature in the Bible.

Apocalyptic literature deals with revelation about the mysteries that underlie human history. (The word *apocalypse* means "revelation.") Although it is sometimes difficult for us to make sense out of human history, the Bible tells us that God has a hidden plan for humanity. God directs human affairs so that they fulfill his eternal plan, or design.

In the Book of Daniel, mysterious heavenly beings reveal hidden knowledge to the prophet Daniel so that the Chosen People can understand what has happened, or will happen, to them. The heavenly beings in the visions encourage the people to have hope for the future—particularly to look forward to the time when God's complete plan for the world will be revealed and fulfilled.

From our point of view, history is complex and full of many events that seem contradictory. From God's point of view, however, history makes sense

as it follows the divine plan: History involves the battle between good and evil, between light and darkness, between the kingdom of God and the kingdom of human pride.

Just as the writings of the prophets contain messages that are not always easy to figure out, so also the apocalyptic writings contain visions with symbols that are not always easy to understand. In his first vision, for example, Daniel saw four great beasts rising up out of the sea. The first beast seemed to be a lion with the wings of an eagle; the second was a great bear that devoured flesh. Following that was a leopard with four heads and four wings. And, finally, there was another monstrous beast that was almost impossible to describe—it had ten horns and teeth of iron that ravenously ate everything.

The prophet then noticed among the ten horns of the beast one horn smaller than the others. However, it grew and eliminated several of the others. This horn had eyes, and a mouth that threatened and cursed.

What was the meaning of this vision? To understand it, it's important not to concentrate just on picturing strange animals to ourselves. To un-

derstand the full meaning of such a vision, the people of ancient times did not pay attention to specific details, but rather they looked at the whole. To them the four beasts were four cruel, repressive kingdoms, probably those of the Babylonians, Medes, Persians, and Greeks. The ten horns represented the power of the various successors of Alexander the Great. The final small but particularly terrible horn was the power of the Seleucids of Antioch.

The most important thing about this vision and the others is the message: The kingdoms on the face of the earth succeed one another, with each kingdom more wicked than the previous one. These evil kingdoms are very different from God's new and everlasting kingdom. God's kingdom will eventually arrive and will destroy all the wicked kingdoms that went before it.

63 Daniel's vision of "the son of man" expresses confidence that God will bring peace and a better future. Christians believe that Jesus was this "son of man."

Daniel's terrible vision of the four beasts rising up out of the sea was followed by another, more comforting vision. In it, several thrones appeared near each other in the sky, and an old man called the "Ancient of Days," with garments and hair that were white as snow, took his place on a throne in the center. He stood for the eternal reign of God. His throne was surrounded by flames, and around it swarmed thousands of angels who served the Lord.

Then suddenly the four great beasts were killed, and there appeared on the clouds of heaven a mysterious human being, who also seemed to be of divine origin. He arrived before the Ancient of Days and was presented to him. The Ancient One then gave him great power, glory, and kingdom so that "all peoples, nations, and languages should serve him; his dominion is an everlasting dominion which shall not pass away, and his kingdom one that shall not be destroyed" (Daniel 7:14).

This vision is the most important one in the entire Book of Daniel. It helps to explain the numerous visions in Daniel. This vision is called the vision of "the son of man" (Daniel 7:13).

Through this vision, the Chosen People learned that in spite of all the evil times they had to live through, God, in his good time, would give them peace and a better future.

In Daniel's time, the son of man presented to the Ancient One represented the entire holy people of God. At the same time the vision pointed to something more than that. Not only the whole people, but one person in particular—a man of mysterious, divine origin—would inherit the kingdom and the power and the glory.

After Jesus, the Son of God, had lived on earth, this ancient vision of Daniel was understood as a prophecy both of Jesus' coming and of his resurrection. Jesus himself would speak of how he would be seen "coming on the clouds of heaven" (Matthew 26:64)—and all his hearers familiar with the Book of Daniel would understand that the son of man was the Son of God. When Pilate was questioning Jesus, Jesus declared that his kingdom did not belong to this world, yet it nevertheless continued to be a part of this world.

64 The Book of Esther tells how God saved his people because of the humble faith of a few Jews.
In this story, Esther became queen of Persia, but the king did not know that she was Jewish.

The Book of Esther deals with a known historical person in the city of Susa in the Persian Empire and with a Persian king called Ahasuerus, sometimes identified with the real-life king, Xerxes. Otherwise, the story has been made up to inspire the Jews. The importance of the book lies in the lesson it aimed to teach.

The basic lesson of the Book of Esther is that God saved his people from great danger entirely because of the humble faith of a few Jews, namely Esther and her uncle, Mordecai. God "has put down the mighty from their thrones, and exalted those of low degree" (Luke 1:52).

The Book of Esther tells a story about a certain Jew named Mordecai, a strong and just man who lived in the city of Susa and served in the court of the king. He had once saved the king's life by discovering a plot against the king. For this he had received honors and promises of further honors.

At the same time, however, Mordecai had made enemies, people who did not look kindly on the success of a foreigner who was a Jew. Among the bitter enemies of Mordecai was a man named Haman, who was already powerful and wanted to become the king's most trusted advisor.

One day the king gave a great banquet to which he invited all the princes, nobles, ministers, and governors of provinces; he wanted to display the glory of his reign and the extent of his power. After the banquet he had a seven-day festival for all the people of Susa. The dramatic ending of the festival was to have been the appearance of the beautiful young queen whom the king had recently married. However, this queen, whose name was Vashti, refused to put in an appearance. The Bible does not say why she refused, but the result was that the king was humiliated in front of all his people.

The king consulted with his advisors and quickly arrived at a decision about Queen Vashti: She was never again to appear in the presence of the king, and her royal place was to be taken away and given to someone more worthy.

A messenger of the king then scoured the streets searching for beautiful young maidens from whom the king might choose a new queen. A number of women were brought to the royal palace to be presented to the king, who would then make his choice.

Mordecai had a very beautiful niece named Esther who was an orphan. Mordecai himself had brought her up, taking great care with her and lavishing much affection upon her. Esther was one of the young maidens ordered to the royal palace. She could not refuse. Her uncle could not prevent her going, but he did tell her for her own good not to reveal that she was Jewish.

At court Esther was prepared for the day when she would go into the king; it was over a year before she was finally presented to him. The king immediately fell deeply in love with her. Thus a beautiful Jewish girl, Esther, became queen in place of Vashti.

The king held another great banquet to celebrate his marriage to Esther. Once again all the princes, ministers, and others came. They greatly admired the king's choice. The king's minister, Haman, would have been outraged if he had known that a Jewish girl had become queen of Susa. Haman greatly hated all Jews.

65 Enemies of the Jews
persuaded the king to order
the killing of all Jews.
Risking her own life,
Esther told the king
that she was a Jew
and tried to save her people.
The king heard her plea
and sentenced to death
the enemies of the Jews.

Haman's power at the court of the king grew
stronger and stronger. Everyone bowed down before Haman—except Mordecai, who bowed down
only before God.

Furious, Haman vowed to destroy not only
Mordecai, but the entire Jewish people, who
seemed to be so proud and certainly so different
from all other people. Haman went to the king
and spoke to him about the plague of Jews who
were threatening the kingdom. They were, he said,
a people different from all the others. They were
rebels and did not obey the laws of the king.

Haman urged the king to have all the Jews in the Persian Empire massacred. And since many of the Jews were well-to-do, their property could be taken into the royal treasury. Ahasuerus, unfortunately, believed all that Haman had told him, and he therefore issued an edict.

Runners took this proclamation to every province of the empire. It contained the instructions that on a single day, the thirteenth day of Adar, all Jews—young and old, women and children—were to be killed. They were to be slaughtered without mercy and their belongings were to be taken. The contents of the proclamation were to be made public in every province, so that everyone would be prepared when that day came. (Esther 3:13-14 TEV)

Thus the entire Jewish people was to be exterminated in the course of a single day. Everywhere the Jews were in despair. They wept and did penance and prayed to God to be saved from the threatened massacre.

Mordecai too was greatly distressed; he went around the city in sackcloth and ashes. Sheltered in the palace, Queen Esther knew nothing of the king's edict until her uncle, Mordecai, informed her. He sent her a copy of the edict and told her to go before the king to ask him to spare her people.

Esther was terrified. There was in the kingdom a law that said no one, not even the queen, was allowed to go into the king's presence without having been summoned by him. The penalty for disobeying the law was death. As it happened, it had been some time since the king had summoned Esther.

Mordecai still insisted that Esther present herself before the king. He wrote to her:

"Think not that in the king's palace you will escape any more than all the other Jews. For if you keep silence at such a time as this, relief and deliverance will rise for the Jews from another quarter, but you and your father's house will perish. And who knows whether you have not come to the kingdom for such a time as this?" (Esther 4:13-14)

So Esther requested prayers for herself from all the Jews in Susa over a three-day period. She fasted and prayed to the Lord, ready to offer her own life for the salvation of her people.

Then she arose, beautified herself, put on her most splendid robes, and, without having been summoned, she entered the apartments of the king. When the king saw her, he held his golden scepter out to her, a sign of pardon and protection. He then asked what she wanted. She requested only that he and Haman together come to enjoy a banquet which she would prepare. The king agreed. And after that feast, he and Haman agreed to come to another the next day.

At the next day's banquet, Esther suddenly begged the king to spare her people. Besides thus revealing her Jewish origins, Esther also accused Haman of having planned the destruction of her people out of personal hatred.

The king was furious with Haman. He issued a new decree that guaranteed safety for the Jews. Haman was sentenced to suffer the horrible execution that he had originally planned for Mordecai.

Following the tradition of the Book of Esther, the Jews began to celebrate every year the feast called Purim. On the days of Purim, they remember how the Jews of Persia were saved from slaughter by Esther and Mordecai.

66 The Book of Judith
is another story
of Jewish faithfulness
and courage.
Holofernes,
an Assyrian general,
besieged the city of Bethulia.

The story told in the Book of Judith* is similar to the story about Esther. Both Judith and Esther saved their Jewish people from destruction.

The Book of Judith is considered to be a historical romance written during the Hellenistic period but set in the distant past. The book begins with a historical error, calling Nebuchadnezzar king of Assyria, rather than Babylonia. This error may have been intentional to show that the story was not meant to be factual history.

Nebuchadnezzar decided to conquer all the territories around him and to destroy all the peoples that might try to stand in his way. As supreme commander of all his armies, he appointed a cruel and terrible man named Holofernes.

Holofernes set out with the chariots, cavalry, and infantry supplied by the king; many camels and mules for transport; and herds of sheep, goats, and cattle for food. Each soldier had abundant rations. With the army was also a large number of men who hoped to have opportunities to raid and pillage.

* This book is accepted by Roman Catholics but not by most Protestants.

This vast army brought death and destruction wherever it went. It destroyed, robbed, and burned. As the army moved forward, some countries and peoples, instead of resisting, opened their gates and welcomed Holofernes with messages of peace. Sometimes they even greeted him with music and offered him golden crowns.

Holofernes, however, was not influenced by their attempts to make peace. He destroyed their temples and then demanded that they worship only Nebuchadnezzar as their lord and god.

Finally the army reached the plain of Esdraelon, in front of the mountains of Judea. The Jews throughout Judea were terrified. They feared for their holy city, Jerusalem, and for the Temple of the Lord.

The Jewish city of Bethulia was located at the point where the plain met the mountains. This outpost could be defended because of the mountain passes around it. The Jewish leaders in Jerusalem asked that the passes around Bethulia be held in order to prevent Holofernes from invading all of Judea.

Holofernes was very surprised when he learned that a band of Jews intended to resist his advance. He summoned the leaders of the surrounding peoples who had already surrendered to him to ask them about this strange people. Achior, the leader of the Ammonites, told him a little about the extraordinary history of the Jewish people, whom even Achior described as the Chosen People. Achior ended by saying that the Jews could not be conquered unless they sinned against their God—otherwise "their God will protect them, and we shall be put to shame before the whole world" (Judith 5:21).

Holofernes was very angry at hearing all this. He cried out to Achior, "Who is God except Nebuchadnezzar? He will send his forces and will destroy them from the face of the earth, and their God will not deliver them" (Judith 6:2-3).

He ordered that Achior should be tied up and left near the walls of Bethulia. Then when the Jews picked him up, he could pass on to them the threats of Holofernes.

Bethulia was a difficult city to capture. But the neighboring Idumeans, enemies of the Jews, gave Holofernes some good advice:

"These people, the Israelites, do not rely on their spears, but on the height of the mountains where they live.... Therefore, my lord, do not fight against them in battle array.... Remain in your camp...; only let your servants take possession of the spring of water that flows from the foot of the mountain—for this is where the people of Bethulia get their water. So thirst will destroy them and they will give up their city."

(Judith 7:10-13)

This advice was followed. Without water, it seemed likely that the city of Bethulia would fall.

67

Judith,
a beautiful Jewish woman,
won the confidence
of Holofernes.
Then one night
when Holofernes was drunk
Judith cut off his head.
Without its leader,
the enemy army fled.

nity and honor. When Judith learned about the condition Uzziah had placed upon God's saving of the city, she went to Uzziah and said:

"Who are you that have put God to the test this day, and are setting yourselves up in the place of God among the sons of men? . . . If he does not choose to help us within these five days, he has the power to protect us within any time he pleases. . . . God is not like man, to be threatened, nor like a human being, to be won over by pleading. Therefore, while we wait for his deliverance, let us call upon him to help us, and he will hear our voice, if it pleases him."

(Judith 8:12, 15-17)

Judith also decided to carry out a plan "which will go down through all generations of our descendants" (Judith 8:32). She went to her house to pray to the Lord. Then Judith summoned her maidservant to help her get dressed up in the jewels and finery that she wore before becoming a widow. Then, accompanied by her maidservant, she set out for the camp of the enemy.

When enemy guards stopped the two women, Judith stated that she was a Jewish woman coming voluntarily to surrender herself to Holofernes. The enemy soldiers immediately fell under the spell of her beauty. The soldiers ended up escorting her to their leader.

Holofernes was relaxing on his couch under a canopy of fine purple material embroidered with gold and set with emeralds and other precious stones. The aides and servants of Holofernes were dazzled by Judith's beauty. Meanwhile, she fell down before Holofernes and honored him. Holofernes raised her up and assured her that she was safe.

Inside the besieged city of Bethulia, the Jewish people tried to conserve their water. Soon some of the inhabitants were dying from thirst. Uzziah, their leader inside the city, urged the people to resist—but the situation was growing more and more desperate. Finally, Uzziah agreed that if the Lord had not saved them all at the end of five days, they should surrender to Nebuchadnezzar.

At that time there lived in Bethulia a beautiful woman named Judith. She had been a widow for three months and always behaved with great dig-

Judith began to speak. She told him that her people now were thoroughly disheartened. She spoke of the magnificent and powerful Nebuchadnezzar, and complimented Holofernes on his skillful and marvelous military deeds.

Judith asked permission to remain, along with her maidservant, as a slave of Holofernes. She asked only one favor—to be able to go out each night into the valley in front of Bethulia to pray to her God. At that point Holofernes would have granted her anything she asked. He assigned a tent to her, ordered that she be given the best available foods, and made it clear that she was free to move about the camp.

After three days, Holofernes gave a great banquet in honor of the beautiful Jewish woman. Judith dressed and adorned herself even more attractively than before, and the heart of the general burned with passion for her. He so delighted in her presence that he began to drink far too much. When the banquet ended, everybody else left, leaving Judith alone with Holofernes. By this time Holofernes was drunk and sleeping on his couch.

Judith got up and went over to the couch. She prayed to the Lord her God. She took down the heavy sword of Holofernes, grabbed hold of his long hair, and cut off his head. She gave the head to her maidservant, who wrapped it up. The two women then went out as if to pray and headed back towards Bethulia.

The following day the head of Holofernes was mounted on the embankment of the city walls. Then the Jews came out on the attack, and the army of Holofernes, leaderless and frightened at the strange fate of their general, fled in confusion. Judith was honored among all the people as the woman who had saved Israel.

68 The Roman Empire continued
to grow in power.
In 69 B.C. the Romans
conquered Syria,
and in 63 B.C. the Jews
came under Roman control.

The last kings of the Seleucids were divided into rival dynasties who fought among themselves. The king of Armenia, Tigranes, took advantage of this confusion and occupied Syria in 83 B.C. The last king in the Seleucid dynasty, Antiochus XIII, fled to Rome and sought protection there.

At that time, the Republic of Rome already ruled over Italy, Spain, Macedonia, Greece, and Asia Minor and was expanding its control. Rome decided to attack Tigranes also. In 69 B.C. Licinius Lucullus, the Roman commander, defeated Tigranes in his own capital, Tigranocerta. After this victory the Romans gave Syria back to Antiochus XIII.

However, Antiochus proved unable to keep order in Syria. So Pompey the Great, successor to Lucullus as Roman commander in the East, in 65 B.C. declared Syria to be a Roman province.

Meanwhile, in Jerusalem, Queen Alexandra Salome had died in 67 B.C., and her son John Hyrcanus II had become king in addition to continuing as high priest. Within three months, his brother Aristobulus challenged him. Hyrcanus finally surrendered to Aristobulus, who then became both king and high priest under the name Aristobulus II.

At that point Antipater, the governor of Idumea, the area south of Judea, intervened in the affairs of Judea by persuading Hyrcanus to try to make a comeback. At that same time, though, Pompey was in Damascus reorganizing Syria into a Roman province, and he was approached by both sides to settle the dispute. He was also approached by another delegation of Jews who wanted to get rid of the Hasmoneans.

Tired of all the confusion, Pompey decided to move against Aristobulus in Jerusalem. In 63 B.C., he assaulted and took the city by storm. He recognized Hyrcanus as the high priest and chief government official, but not as king. Antipater served as the prime minister for Hyrcanus. Aristobulus, along with his sons Alexander and Antigonus, was taken to Rome in chains. This is how the territory that had been ruled by the Hasmonean dynasty became part of the Roman Empire.

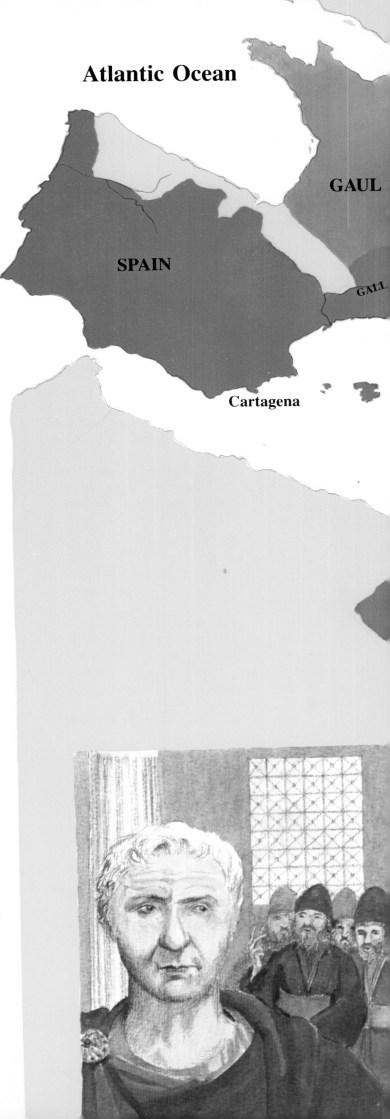

Atlantic Ocean

GAUL

SPAIN

GALL

Cartagena

ARBONENSIS

Marseilles

Aquileia

ILLYRICUM

Rome

ITALY

Carthage

AFRICA

Syracuse

MACEDONIA

Black Sea

Mediterranean Sea

Athens

Pergamum

PONTUS

ASIA

CILICIA

ARMENI

Tigranocer

Antioch

Cyrene

CYRENE

SYRIA

Damascus

Alexandria

Jerusalem

69 The Book of Baruch, named for the secretary of the prophet Jeremiah, expresses the love of Jews for Jerusalem. The picture of removing mourning clothes and putting on garments of beauty shows hope for the future.

The exiled Jews longed deeply for their holy city, Jerusalem. They treasured their memories of the holy city, offered prayers for it, and were eager for any news about it. But the Jews also showed they were capable of adapting to new situations and to new laws and customs, provided those laws and customs did not interfere with the loyalty they owed to God.

The exiles also showed they had a keen awareness of the sins committed by the Chosen People. They realized that they belonged to a marvelous,

Baruch was the secretary of the prophet Jeremiah. He helped the prophet compose and record some of the prophecies in the Book of Jeremiah.

There is also a book called the Book of Baruch.* The book was supposedly written by Baruch in Babylonia, and the writings sent from Babylonia to Jerusalem to be used as readings during worship celebrations. Most scholars think that the book was actually composed by several people who were writing in the tradition of Jeremiah and his disciple Baruch and their followers. These writings show a great deal about how the exiled Jews felt about Jerusalem.

* This book is accepted by Roman Catholics but not by most Protestants.

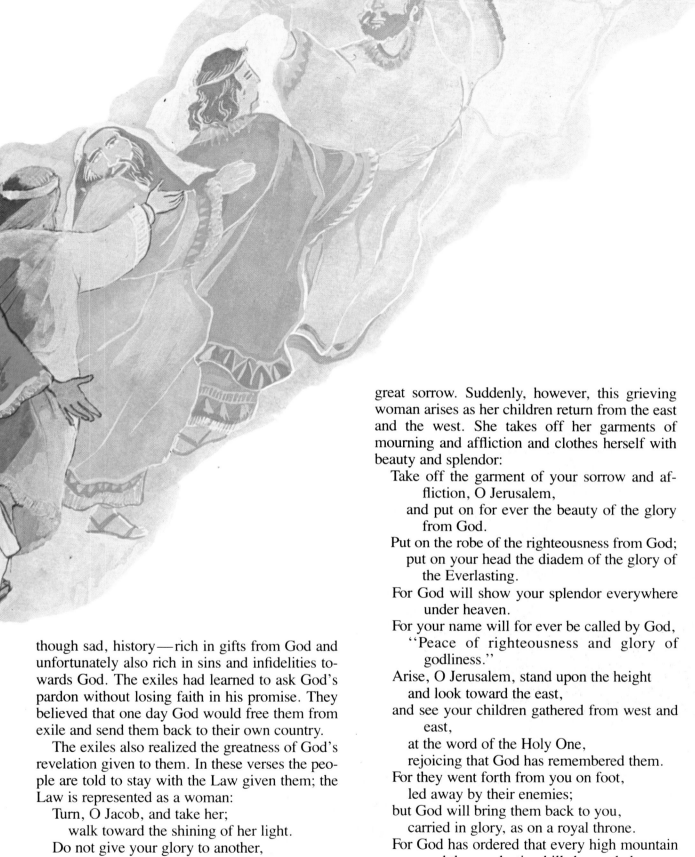

though sad, history—rich in gifts from God and unfortunately also rich in sins and infidelities towards God. The exiles had learned to ask God's pardon without losing faith in his promise. They believed that one day God would free them from exile and send them back to their own country.

The exiles also realized the greatness of God's revelation given to them. In these verses the people are told to stay with the Law given them; the Law is represented as a woman:

Turn, O Jacob, and take her;
    walk toward the shining of her light.
Do not give your glory to another,
    or your advantages to an alien people.
Happy are we, O Israel,
    for we know what is pleasing to God.
                                        (Baruch 4:2-4)

The Book of Baruch was intended to be a book of hope and encouragement. In the book, Jerusalem appears like a woman who has been abandoned, like a wife who has lost her husband, or a mother who has seen her children depart, to her

great sorrow. Suddenly, however, this grieving woman arises as her children return from the east and the west. She takes off her garments of mourning and affliction and clothes herself with beauty and splendor:

Take off the garment of your sorrow and af-
    fliction, O Jerusalem,
    and put on for ever the beauty of the glory
        from God.
Put on the robe of the righteousness from God;
    put on your head the diadem of the glory of
        the Everlasting.
For God will show your splendor everywhere
    under heaven.
For your name will for ever be called by God,
    "Peace of righteousness and glory of
        godliness."
Arise, O Jerusalem, stand upon the height
    and look toward the east,
and see your children gathered from west and
        east,
    at the word of the Holy One,
    rejoicing that God has remembered them.
For they went forth from you on foot,
    led away by their enemies;
but God will bring them back to you,
    carried in glory, as on a royal throne.
For God has ordered that every high mountain
        and the everlasting hills be made low
    and the valleys filled up, to make level ground,
    so that Israel may walk safely in the glory of
        God.
The woods and every fragrant tree
    have shaded Israel at God's command.
For God will lead Israel with joy,
    in the light of his glory,
    with the mercy and righteousness that come
        from him.   (Baruch 5:1-9)

70 The Wisdom of Solomon teaches
that all wisdom comes from God.
True wisdom is seeing
that life has a purpose.

Solomon did not really write the Book of the Wisdom of Solomon, and the real author made no attempt to conceal that fact.* The author called the book the Wisdom of Solomon in order to show the reader that the book was about the same subject that Solomon had made famous—namely, wisdom.

The author of this book was a Jew of the first century B.C. He lived in Alexandria in Egypt at a time when many other Jews were also living far from the homeland they considered theirs. The author was very sensitive to Greek culture, which made so much of wisdom, and, at the same time, he was critical of it.

This author wanted to speak to his fellow Jews, who were disturbed by the fact that Hellenistic culture was so splendid, even though it was pagan. The Greeks had schools of philosophy, strange and mysterious religious cults, and scientific-type knowledge with which the Jews had been wholly unfamiliar. The author of the Book of Wisdom was very familiar with Hellenistic culture and affirmed some aspects of it. Nevertheless, he wanted to demonstrate that true wisdom was what God had revealed to the Jewish people. In fact, wisdom was one of the characteristics of God himself and comes from God.

For wisdom is a reflection of eternal light,
a spotless mirror of the working of God,
and an image of his goodness.
Though she is but one, she can do all things,
and while remaining in herself, she renews all
    things;
in every generation she passes into holy souls
and makes them friends of God, and prophets;
for God loves nothing so much as the man who
    lives with wisdom.   (Wisdom 7:26-28)

In order to acquire this wisdom it was necessary to turn to God, to desire what is good, and to practice virtue. In fact, according to the author, those who chose to do evil did so because they did not understand the true meaning of life. They considered life as only something from which they must squeeze a bit of satisfaction. Wisdom, how-

* This book is accepted by Roman Catholics but not by most Protestants.

ever, taught the beauty of things and the need to prepare for a life that would be eternal. Wicked people were incapable of wisdom because they feared death, and they saw life as pointless:

> For they reasoned unsoundly, saying to themselves,
> "Short and sorrowful is our life,
> and there is no remedy when a man comes to his end,
> and no one has been known to return from Hades.
> Because we were born by mere chance,
> and hereafter we shall be as though we had never been.
> Our name will be forgotten in time,
> and no one will remember our works;
> our life will pass away like the traces of a cloud,
> and be scattered like mist
> that is chased by the rays of the sun
> and overcome by its heat.
>
> "Come, therefore, let us enjoy the good things that exist,
> and make use of the creation to the full as in youth.
> Let us take our fill of costly wine and perfumes,
> and let no flower of spring pass by us.
> Let us crown ourselves with rosebuds before they wither.
> Let none of us fail to share in our revelry,
> everywhere let us leave signs of enjoyment,
> because this is our portion, and this our lot."
> (Wisdom 2:1-2, 4, 6-9)

Evil comes from this hopeless vision of a short and fragile life that has no meaning. People who have such a vision of life feel they may as well oppress the poor and anyone who stands in the way of their getting what they want.

Wisdom, however, consists in seeing that life has an aim and purpose. The wise person has nothing to fear, not even suffering and death.

The Book of Wisdom is a book that makes its readers reflect. It says that there is a deep harmony, or wisdom, in everything that exists and in human events.

71 In the centuries just before
the birth of Jesus,
there was a synagogue
in every Jewish village.
Here people came to pray
and to study the Scripture.
Scribes, or rabbis,
made copies of scrolls
of Scripture
and interpreted
what they copied.

In the second and first centuries B.C. there was a synagogue in every town and village where Jews lived. There were even some in Jerusalem itself, founded by Jewish communities that had returned from exile.

The word synagogue comes from a Greek word meaning "congregation" or "gathering." Usually the synagogue was a fairly large and attractive building with a spacious room in which people could gather. The essential feature of any synagogue was the "holy ark," a kind of strongbox that contained the books of the Holy Scriptures. This ark, located behind a partition, was always pointed towards Jerusalem. When the faithful met for prayers, they also faced towards Jerusalem.

Another important feature of a synagogue was a lectern where the scrolls were unrolled for the public reading. Other furnishings included lamps and seats for the elders. Readings and public prayers were conducted especially on the Sabbath and on feast days. Women attended these sessions, although they were separated from the men by a railing.

The synagogue was never intended to be a substitute for the Temple. The Temple in Jerusalem was unique. Only there was it lawful to offer sacrifice. The synagogue was meant for public prayer and for the instruction of the people through readings from the Holy Scriptures, explanations of what had been read, and preaching.

Each synagogue required a collection of the books of the Holy Scriptures. So the increase in the number of synagogues brought about a great need for copying the Holy Scriptures. This need in turn brought about the creation of a new profession, that of the scribes, to carry out this extensive work of copying. Besides copying Scriptures, the scribes interpreted what they copied. They taught how to put into practice what was written in the holy books. Members of the profession thus came to be called *rabbis*, which means "teachers."

Another thing the scribes, or rabbis, learned to perfection was the Hebrew language. The Holy Scriptures were written in Hebrew. In this period

Hebrew was no longer spoken; the common language of the people of Palestine was Aramaic. The rabbis were able to translate Hebrew into Aramaic as they read from the sacred books.

These translations of Scripture into Aramaic had been handed down orally for a long time. Eventually in the third and second centuries B.C. they began to be written down. These translations were called *targumin*, that is, "interpretations."

In the second and first centuries B.C. many other religious books were composed by various authors. However, these books did not come to be accepted as Holy Scriptures, and they were not read in the synagogues. These works were known as "apocryphal books." Many of them were written by people in what were called "apocalyptical" circles. The people in these groups expected that a sudden, worldwide disaster would occur in order to bring to an end the injustice of the present world.

These people tended, especially after the Book of Daniel, to dwell more and more on the question of universal justice and punishment in the next life. The apocalyptic writers often pretended that their books had been written by earlier authors and had been only recently discovered. From this came the name *apocryphal*, which meant "hidden." Some of the well-known apocryphal books were the Books of Enoch, of Jubilees, the Ascension of Moses, and an additional book named after Ezra.

72 The Dead Sea Scrolls
were found at Qumran in 1947.
These were the oldest portions
of the Old Testament
ever found.
From the scrolls, scholars
have learned more about life
at the time Jesus lived.

In 1947 a shepherd boy who was grazing his flocks in an area near the Dead Sea accidentally discovered in a cave some jars filled with ancient scrolls. As a result of this discovery, other caves in the area were carefully searched, and some additional ancient manuscripts were discovered. Scholars immediately studied these ancient scrolls in an effort to determine their origin.

Then some excavations done at Qumran revealed the ruins of a complex of buildings that had once existed on the shores of the Dead Sea. There were a refectory, where people ate; a scriptorium, where manuscripts were copied (some ancient pens there still contained dried-up ink); cisterns, in which water was stored; and cells where people slept. The coins discovered during these excavations were dated, so scholars learned that this settlement existed on the Dead Sea from approximately the second century B.C. to about A.D. 68.

Meanwhile, more and more manuscripts were discovered in the area. Through these manuscripts it was possible to study the life of the Jewish sect

that had lived there. It was a well-organized community that lived apart from the rest of the Jewish people.

The members of this community lived according to a strict rule. They held their goods in common. They studied the Holy Scriptures and made numerous copies of scriptural books. They wrote books which described their own ideas about God and about how people should live. The members of the community spent their days doing manual labor and studying.

This Dead Sea community expected that there would be a battle between the children of darkness and the children of light. They kept themselves strictly separated from everybody else.

More important to us than the practices of the community were the ancient scrolls that belonged to it. They proved to be important for the study of both the New and the Old Testaments. Many of these manuscripts were of various books of the Old Testament. Some of these were complete books, and others were fragments. These were the oldest portions of the Old Testament ever found. Before the discovery of the Dead Sea Scrolls in 1947, the oldest existing copies of the Old Testament dated from around the tenth century A.D. Some of these Dead Sea Scrolls were closer to the originals by almost ten centuries.

These manuscripts were important for New Testament study because they could be compared with the Christian writings made at around the same time. Through such comparison it has been possible to understand better some of the customs of the times, the meaning of some words, and the reasons behind some of the teachings of the gospels and the letters of the New Testament.

The discovery of the Dead Sea Scrolls at Qumran is one of the most fortunate events of our time as far as a better understanding of the Bible is concerned.

73 In 37 B.C. Herod became
king of Judea.
He brutally killed
many relatives and rivals
to keep his power.
The Romans allowed him
to rule as he wished.

When the Romans made Judea their province, they set up John Hyrcanus II as high priest and leader of the nation and Antipater his prime minister. Anxious to get rid of his brother Hyrcanus and to assume power himself was Antigonus, a prince of the Hasmonean family. His plan for power was helped in an unexpected way when the Parthians invaded Syria. The Parthians were successful because Mark Antony, the Roman in charge there,

During the first years of his reign, Herod greatly feared the existence of some remaining members of the Hasmonean dynasty. Eventually, however, Herod succeeded in eliminating all possible rivals for the throne. Herod made Mariamne's brother Aristobulus high priest at the age of sixteen. But when Herod heard reports that Aristobulus was very popular with the people, the king had the high priest drowned.

Once, before leaving Judea for a meeting, Herod decided to arrange for the killing of the aged prisoner John Hyrcanus II, in order to avoid any Hasmonean uprising during his absence. When he returned, he also had his wife Mariamne and her mother killed. His sister Salome had reported that they were plotting against him.

Herod supported the Roman Octavian against his rival for power, Mark Antony. Eventually Octavian won out and became the emperor Augustus. Octavian allowed Herod's kingdom to be enlarged to the size of the one formerly ruled by

was busy with his love affair with Cleopatra, the last Ptolemaic queen of Egypt. In 40 B.C. Antigonus, with the help of the Parthians, attacked and defeated his uncle John Hyrcanus II and took him prisoner. Antigonus then occupied the Hasmonean throne.

Antipater's son, Herod, feared for his life under Antigonus. He escaped to Rome after sending his family to safety at Masada, a rock-fortress west of the Dead Sea. When in Rome, Herod managed to convince the Roman Senate to name him king of the Jews. Herod then had the task of getting the kingly power in Judea from the hands of Antigonus and the Parthians.

Herod therefore conducted a military campaign in Judea from 39 to 37 B.C. With the help of the Romans he besieged Antigonus inside Jerusalem, defeated him, and handed him over to the Romans, thereby making sure that Antigonus, the last Hasmonean ruler, would be put to death.

In 37 B.C. Herod, then, became the ruler of Judea. To further strengthen his position, he married Mariamne, a Hasmonean princess.

David. Herod was permitted to have his own army, which the emperor could use whenever he requested. Except for not being allowed to make war outside the boundaries of his own kingdom without permission, Herod was master within his own kingdom.

Herod the Great used the generous income from his territories in his extensive construction works. In Jerusalem, this construction work included the royal palace, the Temple, and the Antonia fortress. Outside his kingdom he rebuilt Samaria, which he called Sebaste, meaning, "august," in honor of the Roman emperor. He also dedicated the city of Caesarea, with its magnificent gate, to Augustus.

Herod's last years were troubled and marked by conflicts and jealousy with his children by Mariamne. He had his sons Alexander and Aristobulus killed in 7 B.C. He also had his son Antipater killed in 4 B.C., just a few days before his own death. Herod died in Jericho after a painful illness, and was buried in Herodium, a fortress he had built not far from Bethlehem.

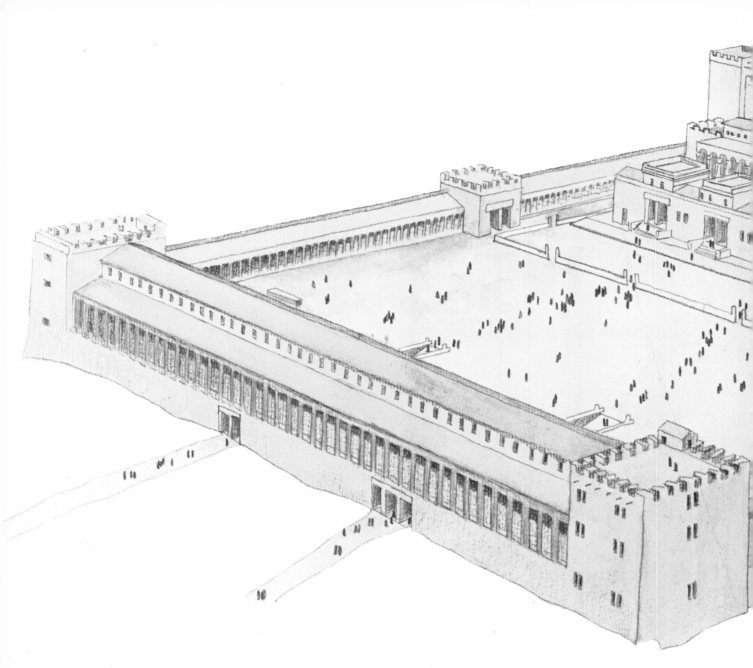

74 Trying to please
his Jewish subjects,
Herod had the Temple
in Jerusalem rebuilt.
This was the Temple
Jesus was familiar with.

During his reign, Herod the Great constructed many public buildings, even outside of his own kingdom. He also rebuilt the Temple in Jerusalem. He did so in order to make more splendid the city to which Jews came from all over the world. Herod also desired to please his Jewish subjects. (Herod himself was not religious at all.)

The most essential part of the Temple, the sanctuary, could not be rebuilt because it was sacred to the Jews. It could, however, be done over by putting a new face of white shiny stones decorated with gold over the rough stone construction carried out by Zerubbabel in the sixth century B.C. There was one problem in this project to be overcome—only priests could enter the sanctuary. Herod surmounted this problem by having a thousand priests trained as masons. He employed ten thousand workers on the Temple in all. They worked on many other nearby buildings and also on new courtyards and porticoes. Herod put up many new structures in the Temple area.

The reconstruction of the Temple area was begun in 20-19 B.C. The sanctuary beautification was completed in a year and a half. Religious services were never interrupted. The work in the Temple area and on the courtyards lasted eight years. The dedication of the Temple was celebrated in 10 B.C., although additional work went on for many years after.

This reconstructed Temple, the one that was familiar to Jesus, consisted of three principal parts:

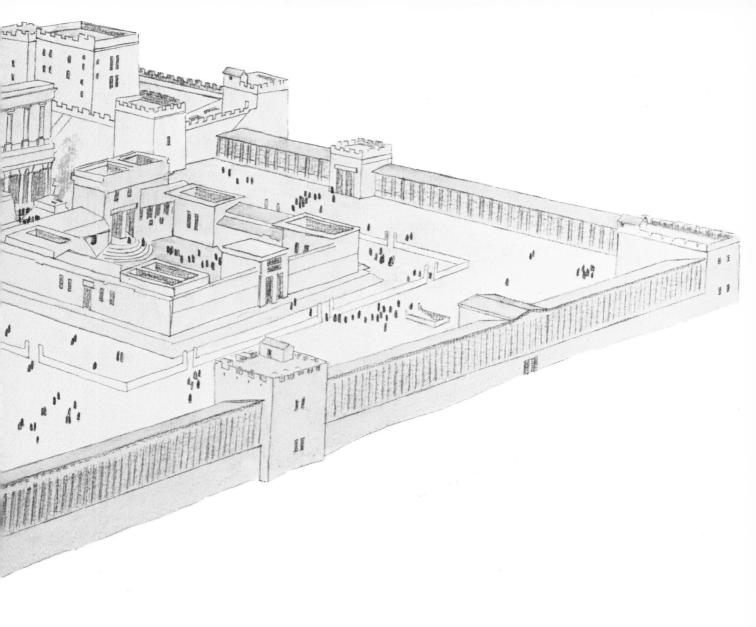

the court of the gentiles, the Temple itself, and the sanctuary.

The Court of the Gentiles. This was the large area, about thirty-five acres in size, that the non-Jews, or Gentiles, could freely enter. In this court, paved with colored stones and surrounded by tall, stately columns, mingled Jews and Gentiles from many backgrounds and walks of life: Jewish pilgrims to the Temple, scribes, merchants and moneychangers—and folk just passing some time in visiting and observing.

The Temple. Rectangular in shape and with enormous walls like a fortress, the Temple had a large entrance on the east and eight other doors along both sides. Inside the rectangle, there were rooms for the various religious services, and several courts: the court of women, and, higher up, reached by additional tiers of steps and a special doorway, the court of Israel (where Jewish men worshiped) and the court of the priests.

The Sanctuary. Rising up in the center of the court of Israel, the sanctuary was about forty-five yards in both height and length. Inside, it was divided into three parts: the vestibule, "the Holy,"

and "the Holy of Holies." In the Holy were located a golden altar for incense, the seven-branched candelabrum, and a golden table for the bread offering. The Holy of Holies, the place of the presence of God, had in the time of Solomon's Temple contained the ark of the covenant. The ark, however, had been destroyed by Nebuchadnezzar in 587 B.C. During Herod's time, the rebuilt Holy of Holies was empty. Only the high priest was allowed to enter the sanctuary and then only one day in the year—the Day of Atonement.

In the courtyard in front of the sanctuary stood the great altar for offering burnt offerings. On the left (to the south), there was the basin for the ablutions (or rites of washing). On the right were facilities to slaughter the animals used in the offering of sacrifices. Solemn religious rites went on there, with the trumpet blasts of the Levites and the smoke of the burnt offerings rising.

75 This chapter tells about
the main themes
of the Scriptures
written during the period
of the Exile and
the return to Palestine.
This was the period
of several centuries
just before the birth of Jesus.

Angels

The word comes from a Greek word meaning "messenger." In early biblical times angels were thought of as messengers of God that communicated the divine will to human beings. After the Babylonian exile many Jews believed that there were good angels sent from God and wicked angels who did the bidding of Satan, the enemy of God. Some angels sent by God to help humans are given names: Michael, Gabriel, and Raphael.

Apocalyptic Writing

The word "apocalyptic" describes a kind of prophetic writing originating about 200 B.C. Writing of this kind uses symbols and coded language to describe an approaching world catastrophe that will inaugurate the kingdom of God. In a final battle the forces of good will defeat the power of evil.

Martyrdom

In a religious meaning this word is applied to giving one's life for one's faith. The word *martyr* in Greek means "witness." Many Jews suffered martyrdom in the religious persecution unleashed by Antiochus IV.

Messiah

This Hebrew word meaning "anointed one" designated a king or priest set apart for a special role. Jews believed that God would send a descendant of David as a Messiah who would overcome wickedness and establish a kingdom where peace and justice would prevail. During and after the Exile the Jewish idea of the Messiah to come underwent developments. Ezekiel spoke of the Messiah as a good shepherd. In Second Isaiah there appeared a new savior-figure called "the servant of Yahweh" who would undergo persecution and death. From the servant's sacrifice sinners would be reconciled to God, and the servant in turn would be honored and glorified.

The Kingdom of God

Along with the expectation of the coming of the Messiah, the concept of the reign or kingdom of God became common in post-exilic times. The kingdom of God referred to a new order of things in which God's rule would be recognized by all peoples. The Jews would be the caretakers of this new order extended to all.

Individual Responsibility

A new theological development occurred through the preaching of Ezekiel during the Exile. He told his hearers that each person is responsible for his or her own conduct and for the results of that conduct. Before the Exile, communities or families felt responsible for the sins of their members. According to this new teaching, the child will not suffer for the evil done by a parent, and the parent will not suffer for the child.

Punishment and Reward

The ancient Jews believed that God rewarded or punished them as a community. If the community as a whole obeyed God, it prospered; but if it sinned, it suffered misfortunes. When the idea of individual responsibility was introduced, a serious and unsolved problem had to be faced: Why do good persons suffer? The Book of Job tries to answer this question.

Later writing, in the Book of Wisdom, begins to show a belief in immortality or life after death. It is somehow less difficult to accept the mystery of God's justice when one believes that final reward or punishment is reserved to the judgment of God after the end of this mortal life.

Outline by Chapter

EXILE AND RETURN